Breast Cancer and
Ovarian Cancer

Beating the Odds

Breast Cancer and Ovarian Cancer

Beating the Odds

M. Margaret Kemeny, M.D.
and Paula Dranov

Illustrations by Mona Mark

Addison-Wesley Publishing Company
Reading, Massachusetts · Menlo Park, California · New York
Don Mills, Ontario · Wokingham, England · Amsterdam
Bonn · Sydney · Singapore · Tokyo · Madrid · San Juan
Paris · Seoul · Milan · Mexico City · Taipei

Some of the material for Figure 5.2 was taken from the American Cancer Society's breast self-examination pamphlet. Used with permission.

Many of the designations used by manufacturers and sellers to distinguish their products are claimed as trademarks. Where those designations appear in this book and Addison-Wesley was aware of a trademark claim, the designations have been printed in initial capital letters (i.e., Krebiozen).

Library of Congress Cataloging-in-Publication Data

Kemeny, M. Margaret.
 Breast cancer and ovarian cancer : beating the odds / M. Margaret Kemeny and Paula Dranov; illustrations by Mona Mark.
  p. cm.—(Reducing your hereditary risk)
 Includes index.
 ISBN 0-201-57783-6
 1. Breast—Cancer—Prevention. 2. Ovaries—Cancer—Prevention. 3. Breast—Cancer—Risk factors. 4. Ovaries—Cancer—Risk factors.
 I. Dranov, Paula. II. Title. III. Series.
 RC280.B8K47 1992
616.99′449—dc20   91-39411
                    CIP

Cover design by John Martucci
Text design by Joyce C. Weston
Set in 10-point Clarendon Light by NK Graphics, Keene, NH

1 2 3 4 5 6 7 8 9 MU 9695949392
First printing, June 1992

Contents

List of Illustrations viii

Introduction 1

Chapter 1. Who Is at Risk? 5

Chapter 2. Is It in the Genes? 23

Chapter 3. Your Body and Cancer 41

Chapter 4. Nutrition and Cancer 59

Chapter 5. Early Warning Systems 76

Chapter 6. Signs and Symptoms 102

Chapter 7. Facing Up to Your Risks 111

Chapter 8. Personality, Attitude and Cancer 122

Chapter 9. Treatment Options 129

APPENDIXES

1. Fat and Calorie Tables 157

2. A Day of Low-Fat Meals 177

3. A Guide to Choosing Low-Fat Foods 178

4. Desirable Weights for Women 182

5. Resources 183

6. Cancer Centers 186

7. Chartered Divisions of the American Cancer Society, Inc. 190

Glossary 195

Index 209

List of Illustrations

Figure 3.1: Anatomy of the Breast   43

Figure 3.2: The Female Reproductive System   55

Figure 5.1: One Method of Breast
Self-Examination   84

Figure 5.2: Alternative Method of Breast
Self-Examination   87

Figure 9.1: Tumor Sizes   134

Introduction

IF you have a family history of breast and/or ovarian cancer, you undoubtedly realize that your own risk of developing either (or both) of these diseases is higher than normal. In fact, you probably picked up this book because you have been worrying about your elevated risk and wondering if there is anything you can do to protect yourself. You are right to be concerned. If your mother, sister, or other close relatives have had breast or ovarian cancer, your risk is higher than normal. Although heredity is not necessarily destiny, it can alert you to potential danger in plenty of time to take preventive measures. This book will give you the information you need to evaluate your own risks and put them into perspective.

Indeed, beating the odds of getting these diseases means facing up to risks that frighten you. It requires learning about the diseases themselves and assessing what risk factors apply to you and whether or not you can change them. You can do a lot to reduce your risk of developing breast cancer and to minimize the threat it presents should it occur. Ovarian cancer presents more of a challenge, but luckily, it occurs far less often. Still, if you have an affected relative, you need to learn as much as you can about the disease and about the new diagnostic techniques that may help detect it early when chances for a cure are best.

This book will provide you with the latest information about both diseases. The first two chapters will tell you about all of the factors that influence your personal risk.

1

You may feel better about your chances of beating the odds after reading Chapter 2. In most cases, even with a family history, chances are you won't develop breast or ovarian cancer. Unfortunately, that is not necessarily true for women with *exceptionally* strong family histories of these diseases. But here, too, it helps to know where you stand. Once you recognize the extent of your risk, you can increase your vigilance and alert your doctor to your need for special attention.

In Chapter 3 you will find an overview of both diseases—what they are, what is known about their causes, how they develop and spread through the body. We have included information about nonmalignant breast and ovarian conditions. We hope it will relieve any worries you may have had about whether these disorders are related to cancer.

Probably the single most constructive action any woman can take to lower her risk of disease—breast and ovarian cancer as well as other types of malignancy, heart disease, diabetes, and a number of other chronic conditions—is to control her weight and cut down on the amount of fat she eats. Chapter 4 explains the connection between high-fat diets and cancer and also contains information about nutrients believed to protect against cancer.

We all recognize that cancer is most curable when it is detected early. Here, too, the responsibility—and capability—falls squarely on your shoulders. Seeing your doctor for regular gynecologic checkups that include a breast examination, doing monthly breast self-examinations, and having mammograms as recommended are the only means available today to detect breast cancer at an early stage. Now that most women with breast cancer can have lumpectomies instead of mastectomies, these exams can make all the difference in the world as to what type of surgery will be necessary.

Women with a family history of ovarian cancer have to be especially vigilant. In Chapter 5 you will learn about new methods that promise to help overcome the most difficult problem ovarian cancer presents: detecting it early, when most cases can be cured.

In Chapter 6 you will find a description of the symptoms of both forms of cancer—including very subtle ones that may signal ovarian cancer months before more definitive signs appear. This chapter also discusses the ultimate in prevention: removing the ovaries and/or breasts to reduce the risk of cancer. Although they are considered appropriate only for women at exceptionally high risk, you may be interested in knowing when and why these seemingly drastic measures are recommended.

Another question that may trouble you is how to handle your personal risk emotionally as well as medically. In this respect, everyone's needs are different; how you deal with your own worries depends on your view of yourself, your confidence in your doctor, and your mind-set. But you may be interested in learning how other women have coped. Chapter 7 contains the personal stories of four brave and resourceful women who have faced overwhelming odds of developing breast or ovarian cancer, or both. In all likelihood your own risks do not approach theirs, but we think you will find their experiences and their outlooks instructive and inspiring.

In recent years there has been a lot of publicity about the effect of attitude, personality, and emotional states on physical health. Can you develop cancer because you are depressed? Does your personality predispose you to the disease? Will a positive attitude make the difference between recovery and recurrence should cancer strike? We take a look at those questions in Chapter 8. You may be surprised by the direction new research is taking.

And what do you do if, against all odds, you do develop cancer? Take heart. Improvements are being made every day in treatments for both breast and ovarian cancer. Chapter 9 presents today's treatment options. You will learn about the surgical choices available for most women with breast cancer, radiation therapy options, and the drugs used to treat breast cancer, including hormonally based substances that do *not* make your hair fall out. Although ovarian cancer presents a greater medical challenge, recent advances in its treatment offer hope, and newer and even better approaches are on the horizon.

We think you will feel much better about your odds of developing—or beating—breast and ovarian cancer when you finish reading this book. You will have the tools you need to reduce some risks and enough information to place in perspective those you cannot alter. As one of the women who tells her story in Chapter 7 says, "Fear is no way to live." She is right. We hope this book will help allay your fears and anxieties and equip you to take charge of your body and your life.

CHAPTER

1

Who Is at Risk?

YOU are reading this book because you know, suspect, or fear that you are at increased risk of someday developing breast or ovarian cancer. Maybe your mother, sister, an aunt, or a grandmother was affected. It is true that a family history of either disease can elevate your risk. (In Chapter 2 you will read about the role genetics play.) But heredity isn't the whole story. In fact, in most cases it plays no part at all. The truth of the matter is, just being female puts you at risk of both diseases. But odds are, you won't get either. Although the statistics are depressing—one out of nine women will develop breast cancer in her lifetime, and one out of 70 will get ovarian cancer—focusing on the negative can obscure the positive: eight out of nine women will not develop breast cancer, and 69 out of 70 won't get ovarian cancer.

Still, facts are facts. The incidence of breast cancer is rising every year, and no one knows why. It increased 32 percent between 1982 and 1987 (the last year for which complete figures are available). In concrete terms the increase means that fewer than 90 women per 100,000 contracted breast cancer in 1977, but by 1987 more than 110 per 100,000 developed the disease annually. In 1991 about

175,000 American women learned that they have breast cancer. Some doctors suspect that better diagnosis—more women are having regular mammograms—may be partly responsible for the increase. But better diagnosis doesn't explain everything. We do know, however, why the incidence of ovarian cancer is rising. This is a disease that becomes more common as women get older so the upswing can be explained by the fact that the average age of the largest segment of the population, the baby boomers, is increasing. More than 27,000 cases were diagnosed in 1990.

In all likelihood, environmental influences we haven't yet identified are to blame for the increased incidence of both diseases. It is important to understand that when scientists talk about "environmental" factors, they do not necessarily mean pollution or carcinogens in food or other products we use. In a scientific context the word *environment* refers to everything that happens to an individual after conception—that is, after the genetic input is complete. Thus environmental factors include diet, smoking, alcohol use, and any other outside influences on health. As you'll see as you read on, researchers have strong suspicions about some of the factors that could play a role in the development of breast and ovarian cancer. But so far there is no "smoking gun," no obvious culprit to avoid.

Where cancer is concerned, it usually is difficult, if not impossible, to say for sure what is to blame. Although we are certain that cigarette smoking can lead to lung cancer, no doctor can predict which smokers will get sick and which ones will puff their way through life unscathed. We all know 80-year-olds who have been smoking two packs a day for decades and seem no worse for wear. (Playing the odds with cigarettes is not a good idea. Lung cancer now kills more women every year than breast cancer. And as one physician who treats women with lung diseases puts it, "If you get emphysema, which kills you slowly and miserably,

you'll wish it were lung cancer, which, mercifully, is fast.")
Our best scientific guess is that some people are born with
a vulnerability to cancer, some genetic predisposition that
lurks inside them like a ticking time bomb waiting to be
ignited. Lung cancer may finally be set off by smoking one
cigarette too many.

An inborn predisposition may underlie all types of cancer.
You don't have to have a family history of cancer to harbor
this susceptibility. Most women who develop breast or ovarian cancer have no family history of these diseases. Medical
researchers who study the incidence and distribution of
diseases tell us that the rates of breast and ovarian cancer
differ from culture to culture, a finding that suggests diet
and other life-style factors are the environmental triggers
needed to "turn on" a biological predisposition to cancer
and set off the process that turns healthy cells into malignant ones. With that bit of background in mind, let's examine some of the factors that have been linked to both
breast and ovarian cancer.

BREAST CANCER

You don't have to be a woman to develop breast cancer. The
disease is rare but not unheard of among men—about 900
breast cancer victims per year are male. What is it about
being female (besides having breasts) that puts us at risk?

The hormones that power the female reproductive cycle
undoubtedly have a lot to do with what goes wrong. Observations of who gets breast cancer and who doesn't suggest that estrogen is somehow involved. For instance, it has
long been known that the risk of breast cancer is lower
among women who have children at an early age, and that
the more children a woman has, the lower her risk. Women
who start menstruating early and stop late seem to be at
higher risk, particularly if they menstruate for more than
40 years. Women whose ovaries are removed before menopause have a lower rate of breast cancer. Clearly, all of

these events and nonevents are dependent on the presence or absence of reproductive hormones. No one knows precisely how the complex hormonal choreography that defines a woman's reproductive years determines her risk of breast cancer, although some interesting theories have been proposed:

The more times a woman ovulates between the arrival of her first period and her menopause may be key to her susceptibility. This theory may explain why women who have more children have a lower rate of breast cancer—they stop ovulating for the duration of each pregnancy. Could it also be that the hormonal changes that occur during pregnancy are protective? Maybe. No one knows for sure. Obviously, a woman whose ovaries are removed before she reaches menopause will stop ovulating earlier than usual. Her primary estrogen supply is cut off, and her risk of breast cancer drops. (In most cases, however, estrogen replacement is prescribed unless a woman can't tolerate it or has a health problem it would complicate. The younger a woman is when her ovaries are removed, the more likely it is that she will receive estrogen. Although estrogen replacement may erase the advantage gained by removing her ovaries, it can protect her from osteoporosis and heart disease, both of which are far more common than breast cancer.) Since the absence of estrogen seems to protect against breast cancer, perhaps years of unrelenting exposure to this all-important hormone sets the stage for disease. If so, it could explain why the risk of breast cancer is higher than normal among women who haven't had children and among those who begin menstruating early and stop late.

The less time that elapses between a woman's first period and first full-term pregnancy, the lower her risk of breast cancer. Hormonal changes that occur with pregnancy may have a stabilizing effect on the cells in breast tissue, reducing their susceptibility to changes that could lead to cancer.

The hormonal upheavals of puberty and menopause may

create a vulnerability to carcinogens. This theory may explain why Japanese women who were teenagers when the atomic bombs were dropped on Hiroshima and Nagasaki have had a very high rate of breast cancer. The effect of radiation on their developing breasts probably was to blame. There was an increase in breast cancer among mature women who survived, but not the dramatic numbers seen among those who were teenagers at the time.

These theories are interesting, but they are just theories. All researchers know for sure is that there is some link between breast cancer and hormones. Practically speaking, there is not a whole lot you can do to control your hormonal milieu. Having a lot of babies early in life might help prevent breast cancer, but it wouldn't be a guarantee (and it's not always an option anyway). It is important to remember that the hormone-related risk is only one of many factors underlying breast cancer. Indeed, according to epidemiologist Anthony B. Miller, M.D., if every woman in the world had a baby before age 25, the rate of breast cancer would drop by 17 percent. That would be a welcome improvement, but it would hardly solve the problem. What about the other 83 percent? In the sections that follow, we'll discuss the other risks, including those you can control.

Age

Simply put, the risk of breast cancer escalates with age. It is very low in the very young—less than 10 percent of all breast cancer develops before the age of 30. After that, the rate begins to rise steadily through the thirties and forties, doubling every five years between 30 and 45 and then edging up by 10–15 percent every five years thereafter.

In 1990 a team of researchers at Roswell Park Memorial Institute in Buffalo, New York calculated and published women's odds of developing breast cancer as they get older. Their figures will give you a pretty good idea of how the risk escalates with age:

Age	Risk
30	one in 5,900
35	one in 2,300
40	one in 1,200
50	one in 590
60	one in 420
70	one in 330
80	one in 290

Obesity

You can't control your age (at least, you can't fool Mother Nature), and there's little you can do about your hormonal ebb and flow. But we have now arrived at a risk factor over which you do have some influence. Obesity increases your chances of developing breast cancer. Reasons why remain elusive, problematic, and controversial. In Chapter 4 we'll discuss the association between diet and breast cancer, including intriguing new findings about certain vitamins and minerals and how they influence breast cancer risk. But the obesity issue is a bit more complex than the question of what you eat. Let's look at the facts first and then discuss what they may mean.

Women who develop breast cancer seem to be both heavier and taller than women who don't. Some researchers think body size plays a role in breast cancer only among postmenopausal women and has little or nothing to do with breast cancer in younger women. Risks seem to be highest among women who stand taller than 5'5" and weigh more than 154 pounds.

A 1989 study by a team of researchers at Queen Elizabeth II Medical Center in Perth, Australia found that women who gain more than 22 pounds between ages 25 and 35 are more likely to develop breast cancer than those whose weight does not increase so markedly.

And an important 1990 study from the F. Lee Moffitt Cancer Center at the University of South Florida College of Medicine in Tampa shows that overweight women who carry their extra pounds in their abdomens have an even higher risk of developing breast cancer than those who are overweight but carry the excess in their hips and thighs. It has been known for some time that so-called abdominal obesity raises the risk of developing gallbladder disease, heart disease, and diabetes, but the Florida study is the first to show its association with breast cancer. To determine whether the distribution of your weight fits the higher risk pattern, compare your waist measurement to your hip measurement. Your risk is normal if your waist measures 73 percent or less than your hips. If it is 80 percent or more, your breast cancer risk will be six times normal. For example, if you have a 27-inch waist and 37-inch hips, your risk is normal: 27 is 73 percent of 37. (To find the percentage, divide your waist measurement by your hip measurement.) But if you have a 31-inch waist and 38-inch hips, your risk is much higher (31 is 81.5 percent of 38).

What are we to make of these odd-sounding findings? One possible explanation for the association between obesity and breast cancer is that excess body fat seems to raise estrogen levels. We have already discussed the theory that the longer a woman is exposed to estrogen, the greater her risk of breast cancer. Simply being overweight may nudge up the hormonal ante and explain the link between obesity and breast cancer.

The fact that height as well as weight appears to play a role bolsters the notion that nutrition is a key factor in breast cancer development and may partially explain why rates of the disease are increasing year by year. Studies of immigrants to the United States show that second-generation

Americans are taller and heavier than their parents. The only reasonable explanation for the change is nutrition—the differences in diet between the generations and diet's influence on body size.

The Australian study also showed that the heavier a woman is, the more likely she is to have begun menstruating early and to stop later. This link further supports the idea that obesity affects a woman's risk of breast cancer by increasing her exposure to estrogen. The researchers also observed that the heavier a woman is, the more advanced breast cancer tends to be at diagnosis. But they couldn't determine whether hormonal factors were responsible or whether excess fat delayed diagnosis by making it more difficult to examine the breast and detect the tumor.

The Florida researchers noted that abdominal obesity is associated with hormonal abnormalities similar to those seen when breast cancer occurs. This complex scenario involves the amounts of estrogen safely bound to certain body proteins, as opposed to unbound estrogen, which circulates freely. Researchers believe that unbound estrogen is linked to breast cancer development. Happily, losing weight restores the hormonal picture to normal.

Birth Control Pills

If you have ever taken oral contraceptives—birth control pills—you undoubtedly have been concerned about recent reports linking them with breast cancer. Not surprisingly, the question of whether the pill can cause cancer has been examined repeatedly in the 30 years since it was introduced. Most studies have failed to find an association between taking the pill and subsequent development of breast cancer. Some have suggested that it may even protect against breast cancer. However, some experts believe that we're just getting to the point where we can gather meaningful information on the subject. The pill has now been around long enough for an effect on breast cancer rates to appear. But oral contraceptives have changed a lot in those 30 years. The hormone content of today's pill is much lower than it was in the original version. We can only say for sure that no evidence exists that attributes to the pill a dramatic rise in breast cancer. Although the incidence of breast cancer has been steadily increasing, it doesn't strongly correlate with the introduction and escalating use of oral contraceptives.

However, a 1989 study by Samuel Shapiro of Boston University School of Medicine indicates that some women who have taken the pill for 10 years or longer have a fourfold increase in breast cancer. This figure sounds alarming, but only a small group of women were at risk: those who started menstruating before the age of 13 and did not have children. Even the researchers who conducted the study expressed surprise at the results and cautioned that they should not be regarded as gospel unless confirmed by other studies. We may have more and better information to go on when the National Cancer Institute (NCI) completes an ongoing study involving 5000 women across the United States. The NCI researchers are examining the interactive relationship of the pill, diet, and alcohol (more about that later) to breast cancer development. Their results should be available in 1993.

Estrogen Replacement

And what about estrogen replacement for postmenopausal women? This is a very tricky issue, and it poses difficult questions. Until recently, there was little to suggest that estrogen replacement affects the risk of breast cancer. But some new evidence indicates that long-term use may pose a problem.

Estrogen replacement has been around for decades. It was very popular until the mid-1970s when showed that it increased the risk of uterine cancer. Almost overnight, millions of women stopped taking estrogen. Since then, the addition of progesterone has reduced the uterine cancer risk, and hormone therapy for postmenopausal women has made a comeback. It is now prescribed to relieve hot flashes, vaginal dryness, and other symptoms of menopause and to prevent bone loss that can lead to osteoporosis. Women taking estrogen replacement also have a lower incidence of heart disease than those who don't, suggesting that the estrogen prolongs the protection that women of child-bearing age enjoy.

Since heart disease is a major killer—it is responsible for 65 percent of all deaths of women over 65 (breast cancer causes only 2 percent of deaths in women this age)—estrogen replacement may be a lifesaver. And since osteoporosis is widespread and responsible for millions of disabling or fatal hip fractures among the elderly, estrogen replacement clearly fills an important medical need among women at high risk of osteoporosis. There's also new evidence that women who take estrogen replacement live about four years longer than women who don't.

But what about breast cancer?

Two recent studies have suggested that estrogen replacement can increase the risk. A 1989 study by Lief A. Bergkvist, M. D., of University Hospital in Uppsala, Sweden shows an increased incidence of breast cancer among women who take estrogen replacement. The biggest increase was seen among those who took an estrogen and progesterone combination for more than six years, but there also was a higher than normal incidence among women who took estrogen alone for more than nine years. The Swedish women studied weren't taking the same type of estrogen used in the United States, a fact that physicians here were quick to note. The difference could be significant and may mean that American women have little to worry about.

More troubling were the results of a 1990 study by a prestigious group of researchers led by Graham A. Colditz,

M. D. of Brigham and Women's Hospital in Boston, Massachusetts that found a "modestly increased" risk of breast cancer among women currently taking estrogen replacement but no additional risk among those who had used it in the past, even when they had been taking estrogen for more than ten years.

So what is a woman to do? That depends on how she and her physician evaluate her risks of osteoporosis, heart disease, and breast cancer. New and better ways of measuring bone density can help predict how likely you are to develop osteoporosis. And periodic follow-ups will show whether the original test was on target. If your mother had osteoporosis, you may have low bone density already. If so, you are at higher risk because you can't afford to lose as much bone as someone whose bone density is higher. Taking calcium and getting regular, vigorous exercise may help, but there is no solid evidence that any other measures are as effective as estrogen replacement in controlling bone loss. You can assess and reduce many of your risks of developing heart disease: high blood pressure, high cholesterol, smoking, obesity, lack of exercise. If none of these risk factors apply to you and you have no family history of heart disease, you probably don't need the protection estrogen replacement affords.

If you are worried about neither heart disease nor osteoporosis, the only reason for hormone replacement is to relieve menopausal symptoms. You are the best judge of whether you need help. If your symptoms are severe— drenching hot flashes that disrupt your sleep and make you miserable, vaginal dryness that is wrecking your sex life— hormone replacement may be worth the risk.

Clearly, more research is needed to give us a better picture of the impact of hormone replacement on the risk of breast cancer. In the meantime, it is important to remember that all of life is a risk. This one has to be balanced against the others that you face.

Alcohol

Yes, there is evidence to suggest that women who drink alcohol are at higher risk for developing breast cancer than teetotalers are. But findings in this area are contradictory and somewhat confusing. The bottom line seems to be that alcohol heightens the threat of breast cancer only among women who have no other risk factors.

The latest word comes from a 1988 analysis by a team of researchers led by Matthew P. Longnecker, M.D., of the Harvard School of Public Health based on 16 reports on the subject published since 1982. Although most of the studies reviewed had found no connection, the analysis showed that on balance the more alcohol a woman drinks the higher her risk of breast cancer. There is also evidence that the association between drinking and breast cancer is stronger among young women, lean women, and premenopausal women.

What is it about alcohol that could lead to breast cancer? The association with the amount a woman drinks suggests that the alcohol itself, rather than something associated with drinking, is to blame. None of the studies found a difference in risk that could be attributed to the type of alcohol the women drank—wine, beer, or hard liquor. All were associated with the increased risk.

So far, no one has been able to identify any mechanism by which alcohol could cause breast cancer. But there is no doubt that women who drink are at greater risk.

Radiation

Radiation can cause breast cancer. This was shown beyond a doubt when breast cancer incidence increased among Japanese women exposed to radiation from the atomic bombs dropped on Hiroshima and Nagasaki.

Other studies have confirmed that exposure to radiation can be a factor in the development of breast cancer. For example, there is evidence that women who received X-ray treatment for enlarged thymus glands when they were babies are nearly four times more likely to develop breast cancer in their thirties than their sisters who needed no treatment. (X-ray treatment for this condition was common until 1957, when it was determined that there is no such thing as an enlarged thymus.) A 1989 study from the National Cancer Institute of Canada showed that women who received repeated chest X-rays as part of treatment for tuberculosis in the 1930s, 1940s, and early 1950s have higher than normal rates of breast cancer. The incidence was greatest among women who were ages 10 to 14 when they were treated; it declined among those who were older at the time of treatment. Women who were 35 or older when exposed to the X-rays had only a slightly increased rate of breast cancer. Higher rates of breast cancer have also been found among women who as new mothers received X-rays for painfully inflamed breasts, a condition known as postpartum mastitis.

Radiation still is used to treat some diseases but not for any of the conditions mentioned. If you have had cancer and were treated with radiation, your risk of developing breast cancer may be higher than normal. But if it helped you survive a previous bout with cancer, you probably have very different feelings about it than you would if you had been accidentally exposed to radiation or had been treated with it for a condition that was not life-threatening.

But what about mammograms, the X-rays used to screen for and diagnose breast cancer? Yes, they can pose a risk—nothing in life is foolproof—but the danger is extremely low and should not discourage you from having mammograms. We'll discuss the subject in more detail in Chapter 5.

Sunlight

Here's good news for Sunbelt residents: Your risk of breast cancer is lower than it would be if you were living in the gray cities of the Northeast. A recent study found that breast cancer rates are lowest in cities with the most sunshine. For example, the annual cancer death rate in New York is 33 per 100,000 women, compared with 22 per 100,000 in sunny San Antonio. Some researchers attribute the difference to the effect of sunlight on our ability to synthesize vitamin D. It isn't a good idea to try to store up vitamin D by sunbathing in the summer: you're more likely to get skin cancer than breast cancer. Instead, fill your vitamin D requirements by drinking fortified milk and eating oily fish (sardines, herring, salmon, and tuna).

OVARIAN CANCER

Many of the risk factors that apply to breast cancer hold true for ovarian cancer. The overlap is striking and suggests that, although they arise in different body sites, a similar mechanism may underlie both diseases. Indeed, women who have had breast cancer have twice the normal risk of developing ovarian cancer, and women who have had ovarian cancer are three to four times more likely to develop breast cancer. The incidence of both diseases also increases with age—up to a point. After 80 the risk of ovarian cancer begins to decline, but there is no such downturn with breast cancer. The peak incidence of ovarian cancer—when the greatest number of cases occur—is between the ages of 55 and 59.

In both breast and ovarian cancer, a family history may be key. You'll find a full discussion of family history in Chapter 2.

Like breast cancer, the rate of ovarian cancer varies from culture to culture. It is highest among white women living in Europe and North America and is lowest among blacks, no matter where they live. In South Africa white women have twice the rate of ovarian cancer as blacks. Incidence is also low among Asian women, although it begins to rise when they immigrate to Western countries and adopt new life-styles and diets. Ovarian cancer is also more common among women of high socioeconomic status. To a degree, affluent life-styles may account for the differences in ovarian cancer rates between the races, although so far there has been no increased incidence of the disease among affluent blacks.

Underlying the socioeconomic risk are two major factors: (1) affluent women tend to have fewer children and to have them later in life than poor women, and (2) affluent Western diets are high in fat, which increases the risk of ovarian cancer. We'll discuss high-fat diets in detail in Chapter 4. First, let's consider the impact of pregnancy.

Hormones and Risk

As with breast cancer, the incidence of ovarian cancer is higher among women who have never been pregnant. The more children you have and the earlier in life you have them, the less likely you are to develop ovarian cancer. This suggests that giving your ovaries a rest—you don't ovulate while you are pregnant—is protective. There is also good evidence that women who take birth control pills enjoy this same protection—you don't ovulate when you are on the pill. Indeed, the longer you take the pill, the lower your risk of ovarian cancer.

No one knows why not ovulating should protect against ovarian cancer. Since having lots of children when you are young also protects against breast cancer, there may be something to the theory that exposure to estrogen for too many years is harmful. On the other hand, the fact that birth control pills protect against ovarian cancer but not against breast cancer suggests that the ovaries need periods of inactivity to remain healthy. Maybe it is the rest—the lack of stimulation—that makes the difference. Or maybe it is the hormonal balance that occurs when a woman is pregnant or on the pill.

Hormonal factors also may account for the risk of ovarian

cancer being higher among infertile women and those who have had menstrual problems, including premenstrual tension and dysmenorrhea (painful periods). A 1989 Stanford University study found an increased incidence of ovarian cancer among ovulating women who had had unprotected intercourse for 10 years or more and did not become pregnant. The researchers couldn't explain why these women were more vulnerable to ovarian cancer. They suggested that an unidentified hormonal or physiological ovulation abnormality that also prevents conception may be to blame.

Diet

We're going to discuss the link between high-fat diets and ovarian cancer in Chapter 4, but recent findings about another possible dietary link deserve mention here. Although results are preliminary and must be confirmed by further studies, researchers at Harvard University have found that women with ovarian cancer have low blood levels of an enzyme needed for the metabolism of dairy food. This enzyme, transferase, breaks down galactose, a component of lactose, a milk sugar. Yogurt and cottage cheese contain large amounts of lactose.

Blaming ovarian cancer on low levels of transferase is premature and tricky. In the first place, researchers don't know whether ovarian cancer affects levels of transferase. If it pushes them down, then we would have to conclude that the findings are completely off base—the low levels of transferase would be a result of having cancer, not a cause of the disease.

How would naturally low levels of transferase increase a woman's risk of ovarian cancer? Researchers simply can't say. However, the Harvard team speculated that women with low levels of transferase who eat a lot of yogurt and cottage cheese may triple their risk of ovarian cancer. They reached this conclusion by studying 145 women who developed ovarian cancer and 127 women without cancer.

They compared transferase levels with the amounts of cottage cheese and yogurt women reported eating. Those with low levels of transferase who ate a lot of cottage cheese and yogurt were three times more likely to have ovarian cancer.

No one knows how many women have low transferase levels. While the incidence of ovarian cancer has been edging up, it certainly has not increased at a rate comparable to the enormous rise in yogurt consumption in the United States during the past two decades, although it may take many more years for such an effect to show up.

Further studies will be needed to confirm the Harvard findings. If they turn out to be correct, women found to have low transferase levels might be well advised to limit consumption of yogurt and cottage cheese.

Talc and Asbestos

Particles of both talc and asbestos have been found in normal ovaries as well as in cancerous ones, suggesting to some researchers that exposure to these substances may increase a woman's risk of ovarian cancer. Researchers at Harvard Medical School have found that using talcum powder on the genital area or sanitary napkins doubles the risk of ovarian cancer. However, other studies have established that talc does not cause cancer in animals, a finding that raises doubts that talc itself poses a risk to women.

One possible explanation for the association between talc and ovarian cancer is that most talcum powder contains particles of asbestos, a known carcinogen. There is evidence that rates of ovarian cancer are higher than normal among women who work in industries where job-related exposure to asbestos occurs. For most women, avoiding the potential risk posed by either talc or asbestos is simple: don't use talcum powder on the genital area, sanitary napkins, or diaphragms.

Radiation

Rates of ovarian cancer were twice as high as expected among women exposed to the high levels of radiation resulting from the atomic bomb explosions on Hiroshima and Nagasaki. There is also some evidence that women whose pelvic organs have been exposed to X-rays have a higher than normal incidence of ovarian cancer. Clearly, radiation poses a risk, but few women are exposed to levels high enough to warrant concern.

As you can see, it is no simple matter to determine the cause of breast or ovarian cancer. Many different risks and combinations of risks come into play. For instance, after speculating about what might or might not be involved in the alcohol—breast cancer link, Walter C. Willett, M.D., the head of the research team that conducted the most highly regarded study on the subject, concluded that it probably never will be possible "to prove beyond any doubt that alcohol causes breast cancer in humans." In assessing your own risk, it is important not to overemphasize any single factor. Some are not worth worrying about because they are beyond your control. You can't change the fact that you are a woman and you can't stop yourself from getting older. If you don't have children or didn't have them until you passed 30, there's nothing you can do to rewrite history. Even if you are still young enough to have four babies before you reach 30 (the number you'll need for significant protection) you may have other plans for your life that you shouldn't give up. Of course, you can watch your weight, avoid alcohol, make intelligent, informed decisions about using birth control pills or hormone replacement after menopause, toss out your talcum powder, or even move to a sunnier place. But don't jump to any conclusions until you've read further and learned more about these diseases and about what you can do to beat the odds.

CHAPTER

2

Is It in the Genes?

WORRYING about risk can drive you crazy. If your mother had breast cancer, if you were older than 30 when you had your first baby, if you drink wine with dinner occasionally, and if, like most Americans, your diet is high in fat, you may feel pretty pessimistic about your chances of avoiding breast cancer.

On the other hand, if you have no family history of breast cancer, if you had your children while you were in your twenties, if you rarely drink alcohol and are careful about what you eat, you may feel confident that your risks are low.

You could be very wrong either way.

Although the strongest risk factor for both breast and ovarian cancer is a family history of either disease, you will learn as you read the pages ahead that there is family history and, then again, there is *strong* family history.

The fact is that most women who get breast or ovarian cancer have no family history of these diseases. And most of their daughters, sisters, nieces, and granddaughters do not face a substantially increased risk of either disease.

Of course, a family history of breast or ovarian cancer

cannot be disregarded. It signals the need for extra vigilance and, in some cases, very careful medical monitoring. In this chapter we will review what is known about the increased risk you face if you have a family history of either of these diseases. But first, we are going to consider exactly what we mean by "risk."

VARIETIES OF RISK

The concept of risk is often poorly understood. As the old cliché goes, "Life is risk," although most of us do not think of it that way. You may dwell on the remote risk of getting killed in an airplane crash every time you board a plane, but most of us realize that the chances of any one plane going down are remote. If we think about it at all, we remember that the risk of getting killed in an airplane crash is much lower than the risk of getting killed in an automobile accident. We know that the rate of fatal automobile accidents is appalling, but we simply don't consider each ride in a car a death-defying act. We correctly figure that our personal odds of getting killed in an automobile accident are extremely low. But no one with a grain of sense would rate those odds as zero.

When you consider your own personal risk of breast or ovarian cancer, you undoubtedly look at the risks we hear the most about: figures showing that the risk of breast cancer in the United States today is one in nine—one woman out of every nine will develop the disease someday. With ovarian cancer the risk is much lower—1.4 percent, or one in seventy. Although these numbers are valid, they tell you very little about personal risk—your own likelihood of developing either of these diseases.

Absolute Risk

If your risk of breast cancer is not one out of nine, or your risk of ovarian cancer one out of seventy, what do these numbers signify? Both figures are measures of what statisticians call absolute risk and reflect the occurrence of these forms of cancer in the general population. Both also reflect the average woman's lifetime risk of developing breast cancer. The key words in that sentence are *average* and *lifetime.*

The term *average* implies that all women have the same risk, which, of course, is not the case. To arrive at an average you factor in all the women with no breast cancer risk factors—no family history and none of the risk factors we discussed in Chapter 1. Then you factor in all those women with some level of increased risk—a family history of the diseases or one or more of the other known risk factors. This would be a smaller group. Last, you give some statistical weight to all of the women considered at very high risk—those with a strong family history of the diseases plus or minus other risk factors. When all of these women at differing levels of risk are accounted for, you can calculate the average risk. Then, because the risk of breast cancer rises with age, you look at how average risk increases as a woman gets older. If you add up the increased risk year by year from age 25 to 110, you will see that the average woman has an 11 percent chance of developing cancer over her lifetime. You would see that the cumulative risk of developing ovarian cancer over a lifetime is much lower, about 1.4 percent.

Sound depressing? Flip those numbers and look at them this way: The average woman has an 89 percent chance of *not* developing breast cancer in her lifetime, and a 98.6 percent chance of *not* developing ovarian cancer.

Reassuring as those numbers are, it would be a mistake to use average risk to calculate your own chances of developing either type of cancer. You can get a better idea of your personal risk from the concept of "relative risk"—how various risk factors affect the odds you face.

Relative Risk

Since all women have *some* risk of developing either breast or ovarian cancer, a woman with one or more risk factors must measure her personal risk against the odds faced by a woman with no identifiable risk. The tricky question, of course, is the degree to which any single risk factor increases an individual woman's chance of developing either disease. And what about those women with more than one risk factor? How does a combination of risk factors affect their odds?

What you have to do is look at the total population of women with, say, a family history of breast cancer. How many of these women will themselves develop breast cancer someday? Clearly, some of them will, but then again, most of them will not. Still, the incidence of cancer among these women will be higher than it is among those women with no risk factors at all. The difference is the *relative* risk.

Assessing your own relative risk is not a matter of simply adding up all your risk factors and comparing the result with the situation of a woman with no risk factors. Some factors count more than others, and some mitigate others. Some you cannot change, and some you can modify. Which brings us to the third category of risk, the ones over which you have some degree of control.

Attributable Risk

This is the risk presented by environmental influences that can be removed. As we noted earlier, we're not using the term "environmental" to refer to air or water pollution, although both play some role in the overall incidence of cancer. We're referring to those things we do to ourselves after birth that we could stop doing—smoking, eating a high-fat diet, drinking alcohol. How much lung cancer could be prevented if everyone who smokes gave up cigarettes? About 30 percent, say the experts. The same goes for diet—if we ate fewer calories and less fat, we could cut the total incidence of cancer by 30 percent. Since both breast and ovarian cancer are influenced by obesity and high-fat diets, we can assume that changing our eating habits could have a major impact on the incidence of these diseases.

But as we noted earlier, neither of these diseases has a clear-cut cause we can point to and say, "Avoid that and you won't get breast or ovarian cancer." And clearly, there are risk factors we simply can't alter. You can't divorce your family to minimize your risks. But by recognizing the impact of family history on both breast and ovarian cancer, you will be better prepared to make educated choices about how to best protect yourself.

IS CANCER HEREDITARY?

The risk factor that matters most in assessing the danger of developing breast or ovarian cancer is family history. A woman whose mother has had either disease is at increased risk herself, but the extent of that risk depends on a number of other factors. The most important of these is the number of other relatives affected. In addition, family history can't be separated entirely from environmental considerations; families can share everything from a high-fat diet to a lifestyle that encourages postponement of childbearing past the age of 30.

On the pages that follow we will be discussing the various patterns in which breast and ovarian cancer occur within families and the measures women at high risk can take to protect themselves.

Is There a Cancer Gene?

Does the fact that cancer tends to run in families mean that a "cancer gene" is being passed from parent to child? Researchers suspect that some type of mutation or damage to a gene may be responsible for the preponderance of cancer seen in some families. In 1990, a research team headed by

Stephen H. Friend, M.D., of Massachusetts General Hospital, identified a genetic defect that appears to predispose to a number of cancers, including breast cancer. This defect occurs in a gene known as p53, which normally helps suppress the growth of tumors. People born with this genetic defect are at extremely high risk for developing cancer. Researchers do not know how widespread the defect is among the population, but they suspect that it may help account for much of the breast cancer that runs in families. Studies are now under way to determine how often the defect occurs among women with breast cancer. So far it has been seen only in families suffering from a very rare disorder called Li-Fraumeni syndrome, in which a number of close relatives suffer from one or more types of cancer. Women carrying the genetic defect usually develop breast cancer; men tend to develop malignancies in the brain, blood, muscle, bone, bone marrow, and adrenal gland. This exciting new finding raises the possibility that someday women in cancer-prone families could be tested for the presence of the genetic defect and take steps to lower their risk. Eventually, scientists should be able to find a way to correct genetic defects, to turn off the inborn mechanisms responsible for cancer development before they have a chance to spring into action. This would be a very important breakthrough, but as you will see as you read on, it would not eliminate all cancer because it would not help people whose risk is not attributable to a family history of the disease. One of the great mysteries surrounding breast and ovarian cancer is that most affected women have absolutely no family history of either disease. Let's take a look at how family history affects your odds of developing breast cancer. There are three distinctive patterns of risk.

Sporadic Breast Cancer

More than 70 percent of breast cancer is regarded as "sporadic"—it comes out of the blue and attacks women from cancer-free families, meaning, there has been no trace of breast cancer through two generations, accounting for all family members: both sets of grandparents, parents, aunts, uncles, brothers, sisters, and all their children.

The tricky thing about sporadic cancer is that you don't know what it means to future generations. Is the cancer the result of a mutation in a gene that already has been passed along to the woman's daughters, making them more susceptible? Or is it just a freak occurrence in an otherwise healthy family? If the victim has a daughter who eventually develops cancer, does that mean a genetic mutation has taken place? Or could the daughter's cancer also be a sporadic case, another instance of bad luck given the high incidence of breast cancer in the population?

The answer to all those questions is, "No one knows." However, most cases of sporadic breast cancer seem to be isolated events. We can draw this conclusion from studies documenting the risks among women with sporadic breast cancer in the family. The fact is that most daughters of women with breast cancer do not develop the disease themselves.

Unfortunately, we can't say yet whether two cases of breast cancer in the same family are sporadic or have a genetic component. At present, however, a woman whose mother has had breast cancer is 2.3 times more likely than normal to develop the disease herself. Given that the normal relative risk is one, 2.3 is not an enormous increase. Take a look at what is known about the risks faced by other relatives of breast cancer patients:

- Women with an affected second-degree relative—an aunt or grandmother—have a relative risk of 1.5, only slightly higher than normal.
- Women with an affected mother *and* sisters have a relative risk of 14.
- Sisters of patients with cancer in both breasts diagnosed

between ages 40 and 50 have a relative risk of 5. This figure goes up to 10.5 if the cancer is diagnosed when the affected sister is under age 40.

- Sisters of women with cancer in only one breast diagnosed between the ages of 40 and 50 have *no* significantly increased risk.

- Sisters of women with cancer in one breast diagnosed at age 40 or younger have a risk of 2.4.

- Women who have a family history of breast cancer and have had breast biopsies for benign conditions that revealed atypical hyperplasia, an excess of normal, healthy cells in the breast's milk ducts (see Chapter 3), are at increased risk. Some studies have shown these women to be at 11 times the normal risk, but others have found the risk to be much lower—4.4 times normal.

And what about the woman with a case of sporadic breast cancer who has sons but no daughters? Her granddaughters *could* be at higher risk if the original case of cancer stemmed from a genetic mutation passed on through one or more of her sons. However, it appears that the granddaughters' increased risk is minimal—as second-degree relatives, their relative risk of developing breast cancer is 1.5. Unfortunately, we won't know if more than one occurrence of cancer in one family is sporadic or genetic until we discover a biochemical "marker" that will allow us to identify people who have a genetic susceptibility to cancer and those who do not. In the meantime, we can only assess the odds faced by descendents of breast cancer victims.

One hopeful note on the subject of increased risk among relatives of women with breast cancer comes from a recent study at Rush-Presbyterian-St. Luke's Hospital in Chicago. The researchers' results suggested that the risk of developing breast cancer among women with a family history of the disease seems to diminish with age. They found that the odds of developing breast cancer are highest among women with a family history of the disease when they are between 30 and 34 years old. After that age, the risk begins to decline, and by the time a woman passes 60, her increased risk has returned to normal. The researchers had no explanation for why breast cancer risk should diminish with age. Clearly, this is an encouraging finding, but it will have to be confirmed by other studies to make sure that it holds true for all women.

Familial Breast Cancer

So-called familial breast cancer does seem to have a hereditary component: two or more first- or second-degree relatives are affected. It is estimated that familial breast cancer is responsible for about 25 percent of all cases. The first-degree relatives of women with breast cancer—that is, their daughters, mothers, and sisters—have *three times* the relative risk of those from families with no breast cancer history.

The most important consideration for women with a family history of breast cancer in two or more relatives appears to be the age at which the cancer is diagnosed. When breast cancer occurs at a very young age—under 30—the risks to other women in the family could be higher than three times normal, by virtue of a familial pattern. Some doctors recommend that the female relatives of young women who develop breast cancer begin having annual mammograms five years prior to the earliest age of diagnosis in the family. The more affected relatives there are and the younger their age at the time of diagnosis, the more likely it is that the breast cancer is hereditary in nature and that the risk to every woman in the family is high.

Hereditary Breast Cancer

The best way to determine whether your family history fits the familial as opposed to the hereditary pattern is to learn about hereditary breast cancer and then determine whether your family history follows the pattern for that type. Much of what is known about hereditary breast (and ovarian) cancer comes from research being done at the Hereditary Cancer Institute at Creighton University in Omaha, Nebraska, by a team led by Henry T. Lynch, M.D. (See Appendix 5 for the institute's address.) On the basis of their work, and that of others, it is now thought that 5–10 percent of *all* cancer is hereditary in nature, and that about 9 percent of all breast cancer fits the hereditary pattern. Here are the characteristics of hereditary breast cancer:

- It develops at an unusually early age, typically 15–20 years earlier than age 60, the average age of onset for breast cancer; some hereditary breast cancers strike women in their early and mid-twenties.
- Cancer often occurs in both breasts; women with hereditary forms of breast cancer have an extremely high risk of developing the disease in the other breast.
- Cancer occurs in more than one generation and is transmitted from mother or father to daughter. (A man can be a carrier of the genetic trait predisposing to breast cancer even though he himself is unaffected.)
- Cancer occurs in other sites in the body, often the colon or ovaries.

Curiously, for reasons no one understands, hereditary breast cancer seems to be a bit less deadly than sporadic breast cancer.

Despite these guidelines, determining if your family fits the hereditary cancer pattern is not easy. It requires meticulous investigation that includes medical evaluation of all relatives—those with cancer and those without—and a close look at the family tree going back as many generations as possible. As you might imagine, it is not always easy to determine how often cancer has occurred in all the far-flung branches of any one family or whether relatives long dead succumbed to cancer and, if so, what kind. For instance, in the old days breast cancer could have spread far beyond the breast before a woman sought treatment, and her death might mistakenly have been attributed to cancer at a site affected late in the course of the disease rather than to the breast cancer that started the trouble.

Given all these difficulties, you need a professional evaluation to determine whether or not your family history of breast or ovarian cancer (or any one of 100 hereditary cancer syndromes) is hereditary in nature.

When breast or ovarian cancer is hereditary, the risks of developing them are enormous. Under these circumstances, you either carry the genetic trait that predisposes to cancer or you don't. And at this juncture there is absolutely no way to find out one way or the other except to wait and see what happens. You can, however, take certain precautions.

What to Do

Dr. Lynch's team at Creighton has developed the following guidelines for women in hereditary breast cancer families:

- Learn how to examine your own breasts and do so monthly without fail.
- Begin having mammograms at age 25; have one every other year until you reach 35 and then have them annually. If any of your relatives developed breast cancer at a young age, begin having *annual* mammograms five years before the earliest age of diagnosis in your family.
- See your doctor twice a year for a breast examination.
- Learn as much as you can about hereditary breast cancer.

Women who face the very high risk presented by hereditary breast cancer may want to consider a drastic step: prophylactic mastectomy—having the breasts removed to prevent cancer from developing. Women from hereditary breast cancer families who develop cancer in one breast may be offered the option of removing the other since their risk of developing cancer in the remaining breast is so very high. However, no one should consider such a radical preventive measure unless it definitely has been established that the pattern of breast cancer in her family is hereditary. Even then, this step should never be taken without thorough discussion and counseling with physicians who fully understand and appreciate the risk. We will discuss this option in more detail in Chapter 6.

OVARIAN CANCER: PATTERNS OF RISK

Until the comedian Gilda Radner died of ovarian cancer in 1989, most women knew little about the disease or their risks of encountering it. In fact, few physicians fully understood the hereditary component of ovarian cancer. As recently as 1981, when the Familial Ovarian Cancer Registry (now the Gilda Radner Familial Ovarian Cancer Registry) was established at Roswell Park Cancer Center in Buffalo, New York (see Appendix 5 for the complete address), even specialists in the field were not sure how common familial ovarian cancer was. Between 1929 and 1970 there were only five reports of familial ovarian cancer in English-language medical literature. We now have a much better idea of how a family history of ovarian cancer affects a woman's risks. The publicity given the Familial Ovarian Cancer Registry following Gilda Radner's death resulted in an enormous number of inquiries. According to the registry's newsletter, more than 600 families with a combined total of more than 1,500 cases of ovarian cancer have now been located. Each of these families has two or more affected women, the criteria for determining whether a familial pattern is present. The Hereditary Cancer Institute at Creighton University also tracks families prone to ovarian cancer and the breast-

ovarian cancer syndrome—which is the occurrence of both
types of cancer in one family with alarming frequency. (See
next section for a discussion of this syndrome.)

Figuring the Odds

Because ovarian cancer is far less common than breast cancer, the risks of a family history of the disease have not
been easy to calculate. One study found that women with a
first-degree relative with ovarian cancer have 3.6 times the
normal risk; those with an affected second-degree relative
have 2.9 times the normal risk.

More is known about the risk of ovarian cancer when
more than one relative is affected. Like other forms of hereditary cancer, the disease tends to develop 10–15 years
earlier in the daughters of affected women. Among families
in the Gilda Radner Registry, the mean age of cancer onset
in the mothers is 60.3 years, but the mean age of onset
among their daughters is 47.7 years.

Like hereditary breast cancer, hereditary ovarian cancer
seems to be transmitted down through the generations in
a direct pattern of inheritance: mother to daughters. But
the unidentified genetic trait responsible can also be passed
through a father to his daughters. This would be the case
if a man's mother was affected. Of course, he himself would
not be at risk for ovarian cancer, but if he carries the genetic
trait responsible for his mother's disease, he could pass it
on to his daughters.

In these families, women with two affected first-degree
relatives have a 50 percent risk of developing ovarian cancer
themselves. In other words, they either have the genetic
trait responsible for the cancer or they don't. And as with
hereditary breast cancer, there is no biochemical marker to
indicate that they have the trait. The only measure of risk
is the extent of ovarian cancer in the family.

Risks are also very high when the affected women are

aunts and grandmothers instead of mothers, sisters, and daughters. These second-degree relatives share only 25 percent of your genes (first-degree relatives share half of your genes).

In assessing your family history of ovarian cancer, it is important to note any cases of breast cancer. The two diseases appear to be closely related, and in fact, a woman with breast cancer has twice the normal risk of developing ovarian cancer. Women with ovarian cancer have three times the normal risk of eventually developing breast cancer. A combination of ovarian and breast cancer runs in some families. This breast-ovarian cancer syndrome seems to be transmitted in the same pattern as hereditary breast cancer and hereditary ovarian cancer. Women from families with a strong history of both breast and ovarian cancer are at very high risk for both diseases.

What to Do

Any woman with a family history of ovarian cancer has good cause for concern, and obviously, the stronger the history the greater the concern. If only one relative was affected, your risk is higher than normal but not enormous. Still, any woman with ovarian cancer in her background should discuss her risks with her physician. You should be aware, however, that many physicians do not fully appreciate the risks presented by a family history of ovarian cancer. Although this situation is changing day by day, it still presents problems. The 1990 newsletter of the Gilda Radner Familial Ovarian Cancer Registry contained a poignant letter from a woman whose doctor erroneously believed she faced no additional risk because her mother had died of ovarian cancer. Here is an excerpt from that sad letter:

> My physician said the chances of me acquiring it [ovarian cancer] were remote and there was nothing wrong with me physically. Further, that no physician in his

right mind would excise the ovaries from a healthy
thirty-six-year-old woman and that there were no other
diagnostic tools available. [Five months later] I sought
help in an emergency room for the unrelenting abdominal pain which I had come to believe was a figment of
my imagination. Within 24 hours of admission I carried
the diagnosis of stage III [advanced] ovarian cancer.
[Stages of cancer will be discussed in Chapter 9.]

As you will learn in Chapter 6, it is difficult to detect
ovarian cancer in its early, curable stages. For this reason,
women with even a single case of ovarian cancer in their
family may want to discuss with their physicians the more
rigorous surveillance recommended for women from families with hereditary ovarian cancer.

Some women at risk by virtue of a single affected relative
may opt to have their ovaries removed if they are having
hysterectomies for reasons unrelated to cancer. Take the
case of Carol, a 44-year-old woman whose mother died at
age 73 of ovarian cancer. In her early forties Carol developed
benign fibroid tumors of the uterus, a very common condition that affects approximately 25 percent of all women
over 40. Fibroids rarely cause symptoms and don't require
any treatment unless they get very large. When they do,
they probably should be removed. Otherwise, if they continue to grow, they can put pressure on the bladder and
cause serious urinary tract problems that could affect the
kidneys. They also can get pretty uncomfortable, particularly during intercourse. You can have fibroids removed in
a surgical procedure called myomectomy (the medical term
for fibroids is *myoma*) or you can have a hysterectomy to
take out the uterus plus the fibroids it contains. (You will
find a discussion of hysterectomy in Chapter 6.) In women
who have had all the children they want, hysterectomy usually is recommended, although myomectomy generally can
be performed regardless of age or child-bearing status.

Carol opted for a hysterectomy, and after discussing her risk of ovarian cancer with her doctor, she decided to have her ovaries removed, too. "With my family history, I didn't feel that I had any choice," she told us in an interview. "I have been taking estrogen ever since my surgery and haven't had any problems at all as a result of the hysterectomy or the estrogen replacement. I just feel enormous relief." One of Carol's two older sisters had her ovaries removed during a hysterectomy (because of fibroids) before their mother's disease was diagnosed. The other sister has had no surgery and does not contemplate it.

If she hadn't developed the fibroids, Carol would have her ovaries—and her risk—today. It is unlikely that any doctor would have recommended removing them to protect her from ovarian cancer on the strength of her family history, which presented some risk but not high risk. Carol's decision is an option for women like her with a single case of ovarian cancer in their background. Of course, you would have to develop fibroids or some other condition that required hysterectomy before deciding to have your ovaries removed in the course of surgery.

Hereditary Ovarian Cancer

Because of the very high risk faced by women with a family history of hereditary ovarian cancer, it is a good idea for all the women in the family to learn as much as possible about the pattern in which cancer has developed among their relatives. The Gilda Radner Registry recommends that any woman in this situation take the following steps:

- Pelvic examinations every six months beginning in the early thirties
- Every six months, a blood test to detect the presence of a blood protein called CA-125 (see Chapter 5), which may indicate the presence of ovarian cancer

- An ultrasound examination of the ovaries every six months (See Chapter 5 for a full discussion of the two types of ultrasound now being used.)
- Removing the ovaries at age 35 for women who have completed their families

The Hereditary Cancer Institute at Creighton University and the Gilda Radner Registry deal with slightly different populations of women, although there is some overlap. The Creighton Registry is composed of families that have been thoroughly studied and found to have a strong hereditary cancer history. When this kind of history is established, all the first-degree relatives of cancer victims are at 50 percent risk of developing the particular type of cancer that runs in the family. Women in the Gilda Radner Registry have a strong family history of ovarian cancer but are not necessarily at 50 percent risk.

The Creighton Institute recommends that women at risk of hereditary ovarian cancer begin having annual pelvic examinations including transvaginal ultrasound (see Chapter 5) and CA-125 tests at age 25. Any ovarian enlargement detected should be thoroughly explored. Most enlargements in young women are cysts that disappear after one or two menstrual cycles, but women at high risk of ovarian cancer should not play a waiting game to see if an enlargement disappears in a month or two.

The institute also advises women considered at 50 percent risk of developing ovarian cancer to have their ovaries removed as soon as they have completed their families.

No Guarantees

Unfortunately, not even the drastic step of removing the ovaries in these very high-risk women completely guarantees that they will not develop ovarian cancer. A malignancy identical to ovarian cancer has occurred in women from high-risk families even after their ovaries were removed. No one can explain why this disease, intra-abdominal carcinomatosis, should develop. Some researchers theorize that it stems from fragments of ovarian tissue left behind after surgery or to embryonic remnants of the ovaries that attach to the inner lining of the abdomen. In women genetically susceptible to ovarian cancer the presence of just a few ovarian cells may be enough to set the disease in motion. Luckily, very few cases of intra-abdominal carcinomatosis have been reported. Although the risk cannot be dismissed, the threat probably is not great.

CHAPTER

3

Your Body and Cancer

THERE are a lot of myths about what causes breast cancer. Dismiss from your mind any notion that it can stem from an injury to the breast or from fondling and caressing during lovemaking, or that wearing—or not wearing—a bra has anything to do with it. Nor can breast-feeding your children protect against cancer or predispose you to it. No similar myths surround ovarian cancer, probably because it is much less common. To better understand how these diseases develop, you need a working knowledge of the organs in which they arise.

THE BREAST

If you have ever been in a women's locker room, you know that breasts come in all shapes and sizes. If you haven't, you may have spent years convinced that yours are too large or too small. It is the rare woman who regards her breasts as perfect, although the older we get the less we tend to worry about how they measure up.

From the outside, the major features of the breast are the nipple and the pigmented area, the areola, that surrounds it. The color of your areola depends on your complexion—

it is lightest among blonds and darkest among blacks. The areola varies in size from woman to woman.

The inside of the breast is considerably more complex. About one-third of it is fat and the rest is breast tissue containing ducts designed to funnel milk to the nipple and lobules, small, rounded structures where milk is produced.

Breast tissue begins to develop even before birth, in the sixth week of fetal life, but it takes the hormonal changes of puberty to set in motion the process by which it matures. The breasts start to "bud" about two years before menstruation begins. By the time she has her first period, a young girl's breasts have reached their full growth, although they may get bigger or smaller later depending on whether she gains or loses weight. The arrival of menstruation signals the end of puberty.

Further changes take place during pregnancy as the breasts prepare for milk production. After menopause, when estrogen levels begin to decline, breast tissue is no longer required for milk production and it shrinks, yielding to fat. As a result, breasts lose their firmness.

BREAST PAIN, CYSTS, AND OTHER WORRIES

Sooner or later almost every woman finds something in her breasts to worry about. It may be only premenstrual tenderness or pain or it may be a lump. A number of benign—noncancerous—conditions can develop in the breasts. It takes a strong woman not to be frightened by any of these changes. But with very rare exceptions, none of them have anything to do with cancer.

Breast pain, which is very common, hardly ever is an indication of cancer. However, any lump, painful or not, should be checked out.

But what causes breast pain? If it begins at midcycle—when you ovulate—and continues until your period arrives, it probably is related to the ups and downs of the hormones that govern the menstrual cycle. No one knows which fluc-

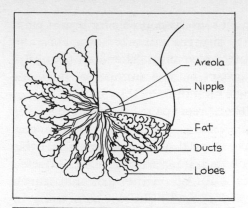

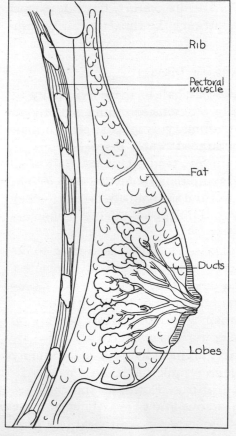

Figure 3.1. Anatomy of the Breast (*Source: National Cancer Institute*)

tuations of which hormones are responsible for breast pain, or why some women are supersensitive to these ebbs and flows and others aren't troubled at all. There is no surefire treatment for cyclical breast pain. A number of hormone therapies have been used, including birth control pills, but not all women benefit. Often breast pain subsides or becomes tolerable once a woman learns that it doesn't mean cancer.

Pain that seems to have no relation to the menstrual cycle is less common and much harder to diagnose. Affected women usually can put a finger on the spot that hurts. (Cyclical pain is more widespread.) Clearly, something in the breast is the source of the discomfort, but it is almost never cancer. Even with surgery the cause is rarely identified.

Fibrocystic Disease

This much-abused medical catchall term has virtually no meaning. Ditto its equally ominous-sounding synonyms: chronic cystic mastitis, mammary dysplasia, benign mastopathy, and cyclic pronounced breast disease. They all refer to the same thing: lumpy, tender breasts. Half of all women complain of these symptoms at one time or another. Usually, both the lumpiness and the pain are cyclical—they show up premenstrually and disappear during menstruation.

The term "fibrocystic disease" has also been used to describe a number of microscopic but perfectly harmless changes pathologists find when they look at breast tissue removed during a biopsy. Only one of these, atypical hyperplasia, is considered suspicious and has any bearing on the risk of someday developing breast cancer.

Although it sounds scary, atypical hyperplasia is simply the presence of more cells in a milk duct than normal, exhibiting some abnormal features. However, the cells are definitely *not* malignant. No one knows exactly what atypical hyperplasia signifies—whether it is a threat in and of itself or a sign that something else is going on in the breast that we can't detect. In any case, affected women do have about three times the normal risk of developing breast cancer, and those with atypical hyperplasia and a family history of breast cancer have almost eleven times the normal risk. Again, please remember what increased risk means— if the normal risk of breast cancer is one woman per thousand, nine times normal means that nine women per thousand will develop breast cancer, not that you, individually, have only one chance in ten of avoiding it.

If you do have atypical hyperplasia, make sure you have annual mammograms and see your doctor at least twice a year for a checkup.

You may also be told that you have fibrocystic disease by a radiologist, some of whom use the term to refer to the dense breast tissue they see on mammograms. In fact, all young breasts are "dense"—they contain more breast tissue than fat. This ratio reverses after menopause when the breast's milk-producing apparatus is no longer needed.

Fibrocystic disease may be a nonentity, but painful, lumpy breasts are real. If you have this problem, you may have tried one or both of the remedies most often recommended: eliminating caffeine and taking vitamin E. And in all likelihood you have found that neither works. Despite widely publicized claims for the benefits of these two modes of treatment, both have been thoroughly investigated and neither has been proved effective. Even so, some women find that cutting out caffeine makes a big difference, and others are convinced that vitamin E did the trick. Giving up caffeine certainly can't hurt you (although heavy coffee drinkers may have a few rough days at first), and careful use of vitamin E (no more than 800 international units [IUs] per day) isn't dangerous. Bear in mind, however, that your symptoms may vanish on their own, as they do for 54 percent of all affected women. And remember that the placebo effect may explain why some women get relief from these treatments. A placebo is a treatment with no real potency that is nevertheless perceived as effective by the patient. We don't know why or how this mind-body connection works. But there is no doubt that some people who believe a form of treatment will help them do get relief. You will find more about the mind-body connection in Chapter 8.

You can also try sleeping in a bra when your breasts are painful. It sometimes helps. So do hot compresses. And cutting down on salt can discourage premenstrual water retention and lessen breast discomfort.

Cysts

Don't confuse the lumpiness of fibrocystic disease with cysts. These lumps stand out. They are what doctors call "dominant lumps"—you can't help but notice them when you feel your breast. Some are huge, but some can be small. Some hurt, some don't. A lump that shrinks or disappears and then reappears over the course of a menstrual cycle is almost surely a cyst. These lumps most often occur among women between the ages of 30 and 50, although they can develop in postmenopausal women taking hormone replacement and, very rarely, among younger women.

Cysts are usually movable, spherical, and relatively soft (they're filled with fluid). You can never be absolutely sure, however, that a lump with these characteristics is a cyst unless you have it aspirated. This simple procedure can be performed in a doctor's office. The physician punctures the cyst with a needle and withdraws the fluid with a syringe. Emptied of its contents, the cyst collapses and disappears.

Although aspiration sounds painful, it usually isn't. Some doctors don't bother with anesthesia, which is given by injection, on the theory that one needle hurts as much as another. Most doctors throw out the fluid—having it analyzed in a laboratory reveals little of value.

If no fluid can be withdrawn, you may need an ultrasound test, which can show whether or not the lump is a cyst.

(You'll find a discussion of ultrasound in Chapter 5.) If it is a cyst, you can relax and forget about it. If not, you may need a biopsy to make sure that the lump is harmless. A biopsy also may be called for if the fluid removed from a cyst is bloody, if the lump doesn't disappear after the fluid has been removed, or if a cyst recurs repeatedly.

Fibroadenomas

The other major category of benign breast lumps is fibroadenomas, solid tumors made up of fibrous and glandular tissues. They usually occur in women between the ages of 20 and 40. For some unknown reason, black women are twice as likely as whites to develop fibroadenomas.

These lumps can be big or little—the largest ones are lemon-sized. Characteristically, they are movable, rubbery, and painless. A lump with these characteristics in a young woman almost always is a fibroadenoma—cancer is rare in the age group most commonly affected. Aspirating one of these lumps won't yield any fluid (which confirms that it isn't a cyst) but can provide enough cells for laboratory examination to determine what it is. Mammograms and/or an ultrasound exam sometimes can distinguish between fibroadenomas and suspicious lumps that could be cancer. If there is any doubt that a lump is a fibroadenoma, it will have to be removed and biopsied. You aren't likely to get more than one of these lumps in your lifetime—if you get any at all. Although finding one can be scary, your doctor will usually be able to reassure you in fairly short order that you have nothing to worry about. Moreover, fibroadenomas have nothing whatever to do with heightening your risk of breast cancer.

Please do not confuse fibroadenomas with fibroids—benign growths in the uterus. Although the terms sound alike, they refer to very different conditions. But they do have in common the fact that 99 percent of the time they are benign.

Nipple Problems

While we are on the subject of benign breast disorders, let us quickly review the conditions that can affect the nipple and may frighten you until you know what you are dealing with.

Intraductal Papillomas: These small, wartlike growths occur in the lining of ducts near the nipple and cause bleeding from the nipple. They are most common in women between the ages of 45 and 50. Removing the duct puts an end to the problem.

Mastitis: This is an infection, sometimes very painful, that can occur in women who are breast-feeding. It stems from bacteria growing in a blocked duct. Massage and applications of warm compresses can sometimes get the milk flowing through the duct. If that doesn't work, antibiotics usually will take care of the problem and allow you to continue nursing (the drugs won't hurt the baby). If an abscess forms, it will have to be drained and you may have to stop nursing, at least temporarily. Occasionally, mastitis develops in women who are not breast-feeding, most often among women who have had lumpectomies followed by radiation, women whose immune systems aren't up to speed, and diabetics.

Subareolar Abscess: This relatively uncommon infection develops in glands surrounding the nipple and can lead to a hot, red, painful abscess that looks like a boil. Sometimes antibiotics can head off development of the abscess, but once it forms it will have to be drained. Unfortunately, the problem tends to recur. Removing the susceptible gland can help, but even that isn't a sure cure. Recurrences can make life miserable for affected women, but the condition itself isn't dangerous.

Most importantly for our purposes here, none of these disorders increase the risk of developing breast cancer.

HOW CANCER DEVELOPS

Your memory of high school biology is probably dim, but that is where most of us learned the little we know about cell division, or mitosis. Normal, healthy cells in the body divide on a timetable dictated by their function, although some are so specialized that they do not reproduce and others divide only as needed to repair injury. The word *mitosis* may have reminded you of what goes on in a cell's nucleus to enable it to reproduce itself. In the nucleus of human cells are 46 chromosomes, 23 from each parent. Chromosomes are chains of genes, each of which controls a very specific characteristic. For cell division to take place the chromosomes must split into two sets, which then migrate to opposite ends of the parent cell, forming two distinct nuclei. Once this happens, the cell itself divides in the middle, forming two cells instead of one, with each performing the same function.

Cancer develops when something goes wrong with this orderly process of cell division. No one knows exactly what must occur to cause a healthy cell to begin reproducing abnormally. Cancer cells do not necessarily reproduce faster than normal cells do, but their development is different and they don't perform the normal tasks of healthy cells. In fact, they have no function at all except to reproduce themselves. If you looked at a cancer cell under a microscope, you would see that it is a wildly distorted version of a healthy cell. The nucleus is larger than normal and irregularly constructed.

BREAST CANCER

Researchers have a pretty good idea of the rate at which breast cancer cells reproduce themselves. Although some multiply very rapidly, on the average it takes 100 days for a single breast cancer cell to divide and become two. In another 100 days the two cells will be four, 100 days later, there will be 16, and so on. With the passage of each 100 days the number of cells doubles. It takes 100 billion cells to form a tumor one centimeter in size, the smallest growth visible on a mammogram. If you add up all the 100-day periods needed to get from one cell to 100 billion, you will see that by the time breast cancer is detected on a mammogram it has been present for at least six, probably eight years. Another two years will pass before it gets big enough to be felt as a lump.

The trouble with breast cancer is that it doesn't always stay in the breast. Long before the lump is big enough to be detected, cells can break away from the developing tumor and migrate elsewhere. They travel via the lymphatic system, a network of vessels and nodes that forms our immune system. The first stop on this trip are the lymph nodes located in the armpit, the axillary nodes. Lymph nodes invaded by cancer cells can swell or harden.

From the lymph nodes cancer cells gain access to the bloodstream and can travel through the body. It once was believed that if lymph nodes were "negative"—showed no sign of cancer—after being removed during breast cancer surgery, the disease had not spread. Negative nodes are still good news, but since we now know that cancer has been around for years before it is detected—plenty of time for wayward cells to escape—finding negative nodes does not always mean that cancer has not spread.

Precancerous Conditions

Since mammograms have come into wide use, we have been finding more and more very early cancers. In fact, it isn't really accurate to call the abnormalities being detected cancers since they can't spread and kill you. There are two types of precancers, or carcinoma in situ (cancer in place):

Lobular Carcinoma in Situ: This precancer occurs in the lobes, the milk-producing structures in the breast. It never turns into cancer itself but can be a sign that cancer will someday develop elsewhere in either breast. We know that women who have had lobular carcinoma in situ have about 7.2 times the normal risk of developing breast cancer at some point during the next 30 years. Again, this isn't as bad as it sounds: if one woman per thousand gets breast cancer each year, 7.2 per thousand with a history of lobular carcinoma in situ will develop cancer.

One of the most controversial subjects in breast cancer treatment today is what to do about this problem. There are two choices. You can monitor the situation very carefully and do nothing else; or you can have both breasts removed (a bilateral mastectomy), which eliminates the danger.

Chances are you won't develop breast cancer—it happens to only 17 percent of all women who have had lobular carcinoma in situ. But if you have other risks that worry you (particularly a family history of breast cancer), you may not want to live with the uncertainty. There is no right decision and no reason to rush. The decision is up to you.

Ductal Carcinoma in Situ: This type of precancer found in the ducts is a bit more worrisome because it can turn into breast cancer, although, again, it usually doesn't. There are no firm figures on how many of these precancers do progress, but indications are that within 10 years of detection 20–25 percent of them will become cancer. There is no way to tell which ones will lead to cancer and which ones won't, and to confuse matters further, there is evidence that some of these abnormalities lose their precancerous characteristics and become nonthreatening.

So what does this mean in terms of treatment? To be safe, some surgeons recommend mastectomy, but if you can live with the risk (a 75 percent chance of not developing cancer), this drastic step is not necessary or recommended. There are two other options: (1) lumpectomy to remove the affected area and some surrounding tissue to make sure no precancer cells remain; and (2) lumpectomy plus radiation, which cuts the risk of developing breast cancer as a result of having had ductal carcinoma in situ to 10 percent or less. With lumpectomy alone the odds become a bit less favorable—10–20 percent. There is evidence that the size of the precancer plays some role in the level of risk. Some doctors believe that radiation isn't necessary for small ones.

Types of Breast Cancer

Does it make any difference what kind of breast cancer you have? Sometimes. Some types are less dangerous than others. However, roughly 70 percent of all cases of breast cancer fall under the heading of invasive ductal carcinoma. As the name suggests, these growths originate in the milk ducts. The word *invasive* means that it has grown outside the duct where it began but does not imply that the cancer has spread beyond the breast. The outlook can be good or bad depending on what laboratory tests show about the aggressiveness of the cancer cells, whether or not they have entered blood or lymphatic vessels, and whether or not the tumor has outgrown its blood supply.

In addition to invasive ductal carcinoma there are several other types of breast cancer:

- *Medullary Carcinoma:* About 7 percent of all breast cancer is of this type. Its name derives from the fact that it looks a little like brain tissue. Although these tumors can get very big, they are not always aggressive. The outlook for a cure is usually good.
- *Mucinous Carcinoma:* This type of cancer, about 3 percent of all breast cancers, gets its name from the fact that it produces mucus. The outlook is considered favorable.
- *Tubular Carcinoma:* Known as "orderly" carcinoma, it is characterized by tubular structures ringed with a single layer of cells. It represents 2 percent of breast cancers and has the best prognosis of any type.

About 10 percent of all breast cancer begins in the lobes instead of the ducts and is known as invasive lobular carcinoma. Its site of origin is the only feature that distinguishes it from invasive ductal carcinoma.

Two other less common types of breast cancer deserve mention:

Paget's Disease: This variation involves the nipple and makes up about 3 percent of all breast cancers. It causes itching and flaking of the nipple similar to eczema. If both nipples are affected, it usually is safe to assume the problem *is* eczema, since Paget's disease hardly ever occurs in both breasts. In addition to itching and flaking, the nipple may burn, ooze, or bleed. When Paget's disease affects only the nipple, the outlook is usually very good. The nipple can be removed, leaving the rest of the breast intact. Sometimes, however, there is a tumor inside the breast. The location of the tumor determines the treatment. If the tumor is close to the nipple, treatment may consist of nipple removal and lumpectomy (plus radiation or chemotherapy where indicated). If the tumor is far from the nipple, a mastectomy may be the only way to safely and practically remove all the cancer.

Inflammatory Carcinoma: This rare variation is bad news—it is the most malignant type of all—but luckily it represents only 1–4 percent of all breast cancers. Symptoms are redness and warmth in the breast, and the condition may be mistaken for an infection. Sometimes the skin becomes pitted like the skin of an orange, a change known as "peau d'orange" (French for *orange peel*). The telltale appearance of the breast reflects the fact that cancer cells have lodged in lymph vessels in the skin, preventing drainage. Even less common than inflammatory breast cancer are adenocystic breast cancer (0.4 percent), papillary breast cancer (1 percent) and carcinosarcoma (0.1 percent).

Location

About half of all breast cancers occur in the upper outer quadrant of the breast, probably because there is more glandular tissue in this area than elsewhere. The second most common location is the area around the nipple where ducts from around the breast converge. About 18 percent of all breast cancers develop in this area. The rest occur elsewhere in the breast.

THE OVARIES

Your ovaries are the size and shape of unshelled almonds, one on either side of the uterus just below the ends of the fallopian tubes. They govern our reproductive process by producing estrogen and progesterone, the hormones that define and promote development of our uniquely female traits and regulate menstruation and pregnancy.

On a monthly schedule, in response to a hormonal signal from the pituitary gland, the ovaries release an egg ready for fertilization. The process of ovulation begins when follicle-stimulating hormone (FSH) from the pituitary reaches the ovaries. As its name suggests, FSH stimulates maturation of the follicle encasing the egg. This phase of ovulation takes about 10 days. Then another pituitary hormone, luteinizing hormone (LH), comes into play. It prompts the follicle to rupture and push its way out of the ovary. The egg then begins its trip to the uterus through the fallopian tubes. Meanwhile, the follicle undergoes an important change: it becomes the corpus luteum (yellow body), whose main function is to secrete the progesterone that prepares the body for pregnancy. If conception does not take place, the corpus luteum degenerates and progesterone production ends until the next cycle. If the egg is fertilized, the corpus luteum continues to produce progesterone, which is needed to maintain pregnancy. Eventually the placenta takes over this function.

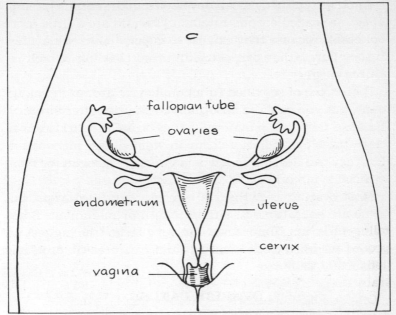

Figure 3.2. The Female Reproductive System (*Source: National Cancer Institute*)

OVARIAN CYSTS AND OTHER BENIGN GROWTHS

Considering the complexity of ovarian function, it isn't surprising that occasionally something goes wrong. One of the most common problems is fluid-filled cysts arising from follicles that don't behave normally. A follicular cyst can grow to the size of a lemon. There are usually no symptoms, although big ones can cause a dull, aching pelvic pain. They often disappear on their own after one or two menstrual cycles. These cysts are usually discovered in the course of a routine pelvic exam. Because they can go away on their own, most doctors will ask a woman with a cyst to come back for another examination in two or three months. If the cyst is still there or has grown larger, surgery may be recommended.

Another type of cyst can develop from the corpus luteum. These are called corpus luteum cysts and are a little more noticeable because they can cause menstrual irregularities. If they burst, they can cause internal bleeding, which requires surgery.

Both types of so-called functional cysts are rarely malignant, but you can't be absolutely sure until after surgery. Because they are functional—they arise in working ovaries—these cysts do not occur in women past menopause. But they can develop in a woman taking estrogen for menopausal symptoms or to prevent osteoporosis.

Most ovarian growths are benign, fluid-filled cysts, but some are solid tumors, either benign or malignant. Some benign ovarian tumors can get very large (the biggest on record weighed 22.5 pounds!) and can present problems because of their size.

OVARIAN CANCER

Earlier in this chapter you read about how disruptions in the orderly process of cell division lead to the development of abnormal cells that form tumors. Obviously, the sooner the abnormality is detected and treated, the better the chance for a cure. The trouble with ovarian cancer is that it usually isn't discovered until it is advanced. It rarely causes symptoms (more about this in Chapter 6), and because the ovaries are located deep inside the body, they can't be easily examined. True, a doctor can feel the ovaries in the course of a pelvic exam, but by the time an ovarian growth is big enough to be detected in this way, it usually has had ample opportunity to cause trouble.

The location of the ovaries also is a disadvantage in the spread of ovarian cancer. Malignant cells that break away from a tumor can easily migrate elsewhere, usually to the other ovary, the uterus, the fallopian tubes, and any (or all) of the other organs in the abdominal cavity. In time, ovarian cancer can spread to the liver, lungs, kidneys, adrenal glands, bones, bladder, and spleen. When cancer does develop in these organs, examination of the cells from the tumors will show whether or not the malignancy is an offshoot of ovarian cancer. (Tumors can be primary, meaning that they originated in the organ where they are found, or metastatic, meaning that they originated elsewhere and spread to the second site via the bloodstream or lymphatic system.)

Of course, the ovaries can be affected by a cancer that originates elsewhere. For instance, there is a type of stomach cancer that metastasizes to the ovary. When this happens, the kind of cancer and its original location will determine the treatment.

Types of Ovarian Cancer

There are three types and many subtypes of ovarian cancer. By far the most common—85–90 percent—arise in the epithelium, the outer covering of the ovary. The other types are either stromal or germ cell tumors. The stroma is the connective tissue that supports the ovary. Germ cells give rise to the ovaries during female fetal development and remain present thereafter.

Each of these principal types of ovarian cancer has a number of subtypes that can be identified on the basis of microscopic characteristics. Practically speaking, it isn't important to distinguish between subtypes, although some studies indicate that certain ones respond better to treatment than others.

Epithelial tumors can be benign, malignant, or "of low malignant potential," meaning that they have all the cellular characteristics of malignant tumors but progress and spread slowly. The outlook for women with this type of tumor is very favorable. Of the malignant epithelial tumors, the prognosis depends on the stage of the cancer—that is, on how widely the disease has spread when it is detected. You will find a discussion of the staging process in Chapter 9.

Stromal tumors are relatively rare—they account for less than 10 percent of all ovarian cancer and tend to be less aggressive than epithelial tumors.

Germ cell tumors are rare, too—less than 5 percent of all ovarian cancer. They tend to occur in young women. Germ cell tumors are more sensitive to chemotherapy than epithelial tumors.

CHAPTER

4

Nutrition and Cancer

THERE is not much doubt that diet plays some role in cancer. But so far thousands of studies from all over the world have failed to establish exactly what that role is. We know that certain types of cancer, including breast and ovarian, are more common in societies where diets are high in fat. They also both occur more frequently among overweight women. Since high-fat diets are invariably high in calories, you can legitimately wonder whether the fat or the calories are to blame. Researchers don't know for sure, and there is heated scientific controversy about which is more important. There are also important unanswered questions about the *kinds* of fat associated with cancer incidence. Are animal fats worse for you than vegetable fats? Are polyunsaturates worse than monounsaturates? And what about vitamins and minerals and their place, if any, in cancer prevention?

Evidence linking diet to cancer incidence or prevention comes from several different types of studies. Epidemiological studies—studies of the incidence of disease within populations—were the first to observe that the rates of certain types of cancer are higher in parts of the world where fat intake is highest. Then other researchers showed that laboratory animals put on high-fat diets develop cancer. In some of these studies, the fat alone seemed to be responsible. In others, the animals also had to be exposed to a chemical carcinogen for cancer to develop. These studies illustrate how difficult it is to make a direct connection between diet and cancer. Usually, two or more factors must combine before cancer develops.

When you consider the incidence of breast and ovarian cancer in the real world, you begin to appreciate the difficulty in determining exactly what factors are most at fault. Given the epidemiological and animal study findings, it is tempting to conclude that high-fat diets are to blame for breast and ovarian cancer. But millions of women who eat high-fat diets for their entire lives never develop any kind of cancer.

Indeed, when researchers recently compared the diets of women who had developed breast cancer with those of a comparable group who were healthy, no significant difference in fat content could be found. Interestingly, the same cannot be said of ovarian cancer. Bearing in mind these confusing contradictions, let's examine what is known about the relationship between diet and cancer and consider how to use this information to lower your risk.

BREAST CANCER

Researchers first began to document the connection between high-fat diets and breast cancer about 50 years ago. Since then they have accumulated powerful evidence suggesting that low-fat diets protect against breast cancer and high-fat ones seem to encourage its development. Population studies illustrate this most convincingly. For example, the rate of breast cancer has always been very low in Japan, where the traditional diet is very low in fat. In the United States and the industrialized nations of Western Europe, breast cancer rates are high—and so is the fat content of the diet. Epidemiologists have searched in vain for other factors to explain this geographic disparity in breast cancer rates, but so far none suggesting that something other than high-fat diets could be responsible have emerged.

, For example, researchers have looked into the question of whether Japanese women might have some inbuilt genetic protection against breast cancer. But their findings always point back to fat. They have learned, for instance, that the rate of breast cancer is highest in Japan among affluent women who can afford to eat red meat, which is not an ordinary component of the Japanese diet. And recent studies have found that as the Japanese diet has become more Westernized—that is, as more and more of the population has become affluent enough to adopt the Western diet—the rate of breast cancer has increased.

Further evidence linking fat and breast cancer has come from studies showing that when Japanese women migrate to the United States and abandon their traditional eating habits in favor of our high-fat diet, their rate of breast cancer begins to increase. These studies have noted that breast cancer incidence is not as high among women born in Japan who moved here as it is among their daughters born in the United States. Two theories have been suggested to explain this. The first is that the women born in Japan have been slow to adopt American-style diets and continue to eat their traditional foods. This theory may explain why their rate of breast cancer remains unchanged or increases only slightly. Their daughters, on the other hand, have a lifetime of exposure to high-fat diets. (Even if their mothers fed them traditional Japanese fare, it is safe to assume that from a relatively young age they have had access to high-fat foods.) Perhaps you need a lifetime of exposure to a high-fat diet for it to raise your risk of breast cancer.

The other theory concerns timing. In Chapter 1 you read that radiation exposure increases the risk of breast cancer most profoundly when it occurs during adolescence. In theory, this exposure would initiate a change at the cellular level that could set the stage for cancer to develop in the future. Something else, years later, would have to happen to trigger the process that causes cancer to swing into action. Perhaps a high-fat diet has a similar effect on young bodies. And perhaps, like radiation, it is less important a factor when exposure occurs later in life. This theory would explain why the Japanese women who grew up eating their native diet, even if they took up Western eating habits as soon as they got to the United States, do not seem as vulnerable to breast cancer as their daughters who were born here.

Animal studies tend to support the notion that the later in life a high-fat diet is adopted, the less likely breast cancer is to occur. Some studies have also shown that obese laboratory mice are much more likely to develop the mouse version of breast cancer than normal-weight mice. And there is good evidence that laboratory mice fed a low-fat diet are less likely to develop breast cancer even when they are exposed to carcinogens that normally cause cancer in mice.

Animal studies also have yielded some interesting findings about different types of fat and their relationship to breast cancer. For example, some researchers have found that polyunsaturated fats seem to make breast tumors in mice grow faster. There is even some laboratory evidence that omega-3 fatty acids from fish oils protect against cancer. Some population studies have found an association between breast cancer and the amount of animal fat—particularly that found in red meat—in the diet. But at this point no one can, with certainty, blame high-fat diets for the high incidence of breast cancer in our society or assert that one kind of fat is worse than another.

HOW DO FATS CAUSE CANCER?

Despite all the evidence linking high-fat diets to the incidence of cancer, there is no scientific *proof* that fat is to blame. The only way to get that proof would be to discover what cancerous changes in the body at the cellular or molecular level can be attributed to fat and what mechanisms are responsible.

So far we only have theories about what *could* happen internally. One theory holds that a high-fat diet—or some component of a high-fat diet—alters cell membranes in a way that may increase the number of hormone receptors they contain. These receptors are like locks that can be opened by only one key. If a high-fat diet does increase the number of hormone receptors, the cell would attract more than its normal quota of hormones, possibly setting in motion abnormalities that lead to cancer. Evidence from animal studies shows that this can happen, but whether it *does* occur in humans as a prelude to cancer is not yet known.

Another possibility: high-fat diets may lead to the creation of "free radicals," unstable molecules known to damage cells. You will read more about these dangerous substances later in this chapter when we discuss vitamins and minerals and the role they may play in cancer prevention.

CALORIES AND CANCER

In Chapter 1 we discussed the role obesity plays in cancer. We are more concerned in this section with an intriguing theory that, as far as cancer is concerned, the high number of calories in our diets is more important than the fat content. Support for this theory comes from experiments with laboratory rats fed a diet 25 percent lower in calories—but not lower in fat—than the meals lab rats usually consume. The underfed, underweight rats develop cancer much less frequently than normal-weight rats who aren't on a low-calorie diet. David M. Klurfeld, Ph.D., of Philadelphia's Wistar Institute notes that thin people—who presumably don't take in as many calories as overweight people—have a lower rate of cancer of all kinds. And studies in humans have shown a positive association between high-calorie diets and breast cancer. Indeed, when the American Cancer Society looked into the question of body weight and cancer incidence in general (not just breast or ovarian cancer), it found that women at lowest risk weighed from 20 percent below to 10 percent above the average for their height and age.

Although it is true that high-fat diets are inevitably high-calorie diets (fats contain nine calories per gram, compared with only four calories per gram for carbohydrates and protein), there is no biological proof that the amount of fat in Western diets is to blame for the higher rates of breast and ovarian cancer. Those who suspect that calories, not fat, pose the greatest risk theorize that chemical carcinogens may be stored in body fat for eventual mobilization and transport to target tissues.

Another hypothesis holds that cell growth is controlled by the supply of available energy and that excess energy (i.e., excess body fat due to a high-calorie diet) may increase cell multiplication and either set in motion or speed up the process by which cancer develops.

The theory that would best explain how high-calorie diets influence breast and ovarian cancer holds that metabolism of hormones in body fat (see Chapter 1) could play a role in the formation and growth of tumors.

David Klurfeld suspects that our high-calorie, high-fat diets may set the stage for cancer by promoting a rapid rate of growth in childhood and adolescence. There is no doubt that a link exists between nutrition and puberty. In well-nourished Western societies, girls begin to menstruate at a younger age than they do in societies where food is less plentiful and nourishing. This means, of course, that their estrogen levels rise earlier in life, a fact that may explain the higher risk of breast and ovarian cancer faced by women in affluent societies.

HOW MUCH IS TOO MUCH?

It is one thing to conclude on the basis of the accumulating evidence that high-fat or high-calorie diets bear a significant part of the responsibility for the incidence of breast cancer in the United States, and another to figure out what to do about it. Should we cut our fat consumption way down, say, from the current average of 40 percent of daily calories to 30 percent or less? That's a tough question to answer.

Consider the results of a major study conducted by researchers at Harvard Medical School of how the fat content of the diet affected the incidence of breast cancer among a group of 89,538 nurses over four years. During that period of time 601 of the nurses developed breast cancer. Did the ones who consumed less fat do any better than those who consumed the most? Not among the women in this study.

On the basis of these findings, Walter C. Willett, M.D., the Harvard epidemiologist who headed the research team, concluded that cutting back moderately on fat isn't likely to do a lot of good in reducing the risk of breast cancer. Discouraging news indeed, but as Willett himself admits, the study had its limitations. In the first place, there was not a whole lot of difference in the amount of fat the nurses consumed: it ranged between 32 and 44 percent of daily calories. Where breast cancer is concerned, 32 percent of calories might be much too much fat. Remember the Japanese women we discussed earlier, the ones who maintained a traditional Japanese diet? The fat content of that diet is extremely low, probably between 10 and 15 percent of daily calories. Now that's low-fat!

We simply don't know whether cutting way back on fat consumption—say, to 20 percent or less of daily calories—will do any good because no one has ever studied the subject. We do know, however, that drastically reducing the amount of fat in the diet can affect the course of heart disease. In one study, heart patients with coronary artery blockages cut their fat intake to 8 percent of total calories and followed medical advice to quit smoking, exercise regularly, and do yoga and meditate to reduce stress. This drastic regime worked: at the end of the study, their blockages were not as severe as they had been at the outset. Of course, we know more about the contribution of dietary fat to heart disease than we do about how high-fat diets might lead to breast cancer. And clearly, we won't know if limiting fat consumption reduces the risk of breast cancer until we try it and see if it works. At the moment, the National Cancer Institute is in the midst of a study to determine whether a low-fat diet will reduce the recurrence rate among women already treated for breast cancer.

For some time NCI has been trying to design a study that would tell us whether a low-fat diet helps prevent breast cancer, but it has encountered formidable obstacles. NCI would have to recruit two large groups: (1) women who agree to drastically limit fat consumption to 20 percent or less of daily calories, and (2) women who continue eating normally. You can see how difficult this would be: sticking to a very low-fat diet is hard. It would mean learning a whole new way of eating, and since this would be a scientific study that could yield precious, possibly life-saving information, it would also mean no cheating. For 10 years!

And what about the control group? Their job sounds easy—they would just continue eating as usual. But what if some of those women decide they want to lose weight? If you have ever been on a diet, you know that the ones that work best require cutting way down on fat. Wouldn't the weight loss efforts of these volunteers skew the study results?

And how would researchers know for sure that the women were complying with their assigned diets? The handiest way to verify their word would be to test them for a marker in the blood that shows whether they really are sticking to their diets. Unfortunately, no such marker exists, so researchers would have to accept the volunteers' assurance that they weren't cheating.

Pilot studies have demonstrated that committed women can stick to strict low-fat diets. In 1990 researchers at two Texas institutions, Baylor College of Medicine and the Methodist Hospital in Houston, reported that a group of women considered at above-average risk for breast cancer, aged 45 to 59, cut their fat intakes in half to 20 percent of their daily calories and maintained the change for at least two years. It is too soon to tell whether their new way of eating will protect them from breast cancer, but the doctors conducting the study reported that the women lost an average of 6.2 pounds and their cholesterol dropped, too. Most of the women reduced their fat intake by cutting down on fats and oils, red meats, and whole-milk dairy products. According to the research team, the women "made these changes by means of readily available foods" and did not have to go to extraordinary lengths to change their diets.

A large-scale study of the effect of low-fat eating on breast cancer risk would have to take into consideration the possibility that the breast cancer risk posed by a high-fat diet develops early in life and can't be changed in adulthood. If you have been eating a high-fat diet since childhood, it may be too late to avoid breast cancer by changing your ways. And then again, it may not. We simply don't know. One thing is certain though: cutting down on fat can't hurt you. It *may* protect you from breast cancer, and it *can* lower your risk of heart disease, a much bigger threat to us all. If you are overweight, it will help you reduce. In fact, extra pounds are *all* you stand to lose by cutting down on fat. If you don't develop breast cancer, you will never know whether or not your new way of eating did the trick. But if you beat the odds, who cares what did it?

*   *   *

OVARIAN CANCER

Evidence connecting ovarian cancer to fat consumption comes principally from epidemiological studies (as opposed to studies on individuals) showing that, like breast cancer, ovarian cancer is more prevalent in affluent societies where diets are high in fat. But some of the evidence about ovarian cancer does suggest that women may be able to alter their personal risks by changing their eating habits. Consider the results of a 1984 study from Harvard Medical School comparing women with ovarian cancer with a similar group of healthy women. They showed that the more fat a woman consumes, the more likely she is to develop ovarian cancer. This is a finding that simply hasn't emerged from studies of women with breast cancer. Remember the nurses? No difference in fat consumption could explain why some developed breast cancer and the others didn't.

The ovarian cancer study team (one member of the team was the same, very busy, Dr. Walter Willett who later supervised the nurses' study) looked at all the women's consumption of fat, alcohol, and coffee and at their smoking habits. The only significant difference to emerge was that the women with ovarian cancer were more likely to use whole milk and butter and less likely to consume skim milk, margarine, and fish. After weighing all other risk factors, the researchers concluded that there was a "significant trend toward increasing risk of ovarian cancer with increasing consumption of animal fat." The women who ate the most animal fat had twice the risk of the women who consumed the least animal fat.

No one knows how diets high in animal fats could promote development of ovarian cancer, but the researchers suggested several possibilities:

- A high-fat diet may promote tumor development by stimulating extra estrogen production.

- A high-fat diet may affect secretion of hormones by the pituitary gland, setting the hormonal stage for cancer development.
- Diets high in animal fats may contain carcinogens known to cause ovarian cancer in laboratory animals.

All this speculation on how high-fat diets may lead to ovarian cancer is just that—speculation. No one knows for sure how it happens. But clearly, there is some link and, it would seem, yet another reason to cut back on fat consumption.

WHERE'S THE FAT?

About 40 percent of the calories Americans consume every day come from fat. Our diet contains three principal types of fat—saturated, polyunsaturated, and monounsaturated. Here is a rundown on how these fats differ and what foods contain them:

Saturated Fat: In general, saturated fats come from meats, dairy products, and other foods derived from animals. We get most of our dietary cholesterol from these foods. A few fats from plant sources are also saturated—you may have heard these described as "tropical oils." They include cocoa butter, coconut, palm, and palm-kernel oils and are found principally in commercially baked goods. To cut down on saturated fats, you should avoid the following foods:

- Red meat, primarily "prime" grade meats, short ribs, spare ribs, rib-eye roast or steak
- Pastrami, corned beef, frankfurters, sausage, bacon, and luncheon meats
- Goose and duck
- Organ meats, including brains, chitterlings, gizzard, heart, kidney, sweetbreads, and pork maws
- Liver
- Butter and other fats from animal products, including bacon drippings, ham hocks, lard, and salt pork

- Gravies made from meat drippings
- Whole milk, cream, half-and-half, buttermilk, yogurt made from whole milk, condensed milk, evaporated milk, and ice cream
- Most natural and processed cheeses (see Appendix 3 for a list of low-fat cheeses)
- Egg yolks
- Cream soups and cream sauces

Monounsaturated Fat: The principal sources of mono-unsaturated fats are olive and canola oils, which most often appear in salad dressings and cooking oils.

Polyunsaturated Fat: These fats are found in corn, saf-flower, sunflower, soybean, and cottonseed oil and, like the monounsaturates, are used primarily for cooking and salad dressing (including most commercially prepared mayon-naise), but they are also used to make margarine.

Fish Oil: Also known as omega-3 oil, this fat found in fish is polyunsaturated. There is some evidence that it may pro-tect against heart disease, and several studies have sug-gested that it may also protect against breast cancer, though more research is needed to confirm these early find-ings.

HOW TO AVOID FAT

Cutting down on fat really does mean learning a whole new way of eating. Appendix 1 lists the fat content of a vast array of foods and will help you distinguish high-fat from low-fat foods. Essentially, a low-fat diet means cutting back on meats and dairy products and emphasizing fruits, veg-etables, and grains, all of which are fat-free when cooked and served without added fat.

You can calculate the percentage of fat in your diet with the help of a detailed calorie counter than includes grams of fat in each food. Every gram of fat provides nine calories, so to see how many calories you are getting from fat you must multiply your total fat intake by nine. Then compare the result with your total calories for the day. If total calories from fat exceed 20 percent of your total daily calories, you have a high-fat diet.

Other hints:

- Avoid fried foods—they are all high in fat.
- Bake, poach, or broil fish, chicken, and other meat. Microwaving is a good way to cook fish as long as you do not add fat.
- Use lemon juice or flavored vinegars as salad dressings; as an alternative, make salad dressing with low-fat yogurt instead of mayonnaise and other fats.
- Read labels carefully to find hidden fats in commercially prepared foods. Almost all baked goods and pastries are high in fat.
- Almost all snack foods (including potato chips, corn chips, and nuts) are high in fat; low-fat alternatives include air-popped popcorn and pretzels.
- Avoid buying frozen vegetables cooked in butter or prepared with cream sauces.

VITAMINS AND MINERALS

Can vitamins and minerals protect you against breast or ovarian cancer? The evidence here is much sketchier than the findings linking both diseases with high-fat diets. But there is some reason to think that bolstering your intake of certain vitamins may reduce your risk of all types of cancer, and a number of studies have suggested that the mineral selenium may protect against breast cancer. That notion was seriously challenged, however, by the findings from the Harvard nurses' health study.

The Selenium Story

The Harvard team decided to check out the selenium story— would nurses with higher selenium levels in their blood develop breast cancer less often than those with low blood levels of selenium?

The idea that selenium may be protective comes from animal studies showing that selenium can protect lab mice against breast cancer and can also inhibit the growth of breast tumors in mice. Other studies had noted that women living in areas with high soil concentrations of selenium have a lower rate of breast cancer than women in areas where selenium levels in the soil are low. And when researchers compared breast cancer patients with healthy women, they found that blood levels of selenium were lower in the women with cancer.

To get a better handle on selenium's role in breast cancer, the Harvard researchers asked the nurses for toenail clippings, the best available indication of long-term exposure to selenium. The researchers then looked at a number of factors that could influence selenium stores, such as smoking and alcohol consumption. After accounting for all the factors in addition to selenium that could influence a woman's risk of breast cancer, they found no difference in selenium levels between nurses who did develop breast cancer and those who didn't. The study probably isn't the last word on the subject. The researchers conceded that selenium intake early in life—which they simply could not measure—may affect a woman's risk of breast cancer. But they found nothing to suggest that selenium intake in adulthood influences a woman's risk of breast cancer.

Vitamin A and Beta Carotene

Of all the so-called anticancer vitamins, only one, vitamin A, and its precursor, beta carotene, has been linked to a reduced incidence of breast cancer. Although evidence is scanty, some studies have shown that breast cancer rates are higher among women whose diets are low in foods containing vitamin A and beta carotene. There is also evidence that vitamin A protects against breast cancer in animals.

How? The mechanisms aren't clear, but laboratory studies have shown that vitamin A can inhibit the process of carcinogenesis (the development of cancer). Beta carotene's role is a little more complex. To understand it, you have to know a little about those dangerous substances, free radicals. Some of these high-energy atoms are made spontaneously in our bodies. They contain an odd number of electrons and can damage body tissues when they throw off the extra electron. This damage can lead to cancer.

Free radicals can also be formed when oxygen atoms split into a form called singlet oxygen, which can cause cancer and activate carcinogens in the body. The interaction between oxygen and polyunsaturated fats in the body can also lead to free radical formation.

Certain nutrients, including beta carotene, have an anti-oxidant effect that enables them to neutralize free radicals. In theory, the more anti-oxidant nutrients you consume, the less threatened you are by free radicals.

The best food sources of vitamin A are liver, cod liver oil, whitefish, and crab. Foods high in beta carotene include carrot juice and carrots (you get more beta carotene out of cooked carrots than raw ones), spinach, mangoes, apricots, broccoli (cooked), winter squash, pumpkin, cantaloupe, watermelon, prunes, and peaches.

Vitamins C and E

Both vitamins C and E have an anti-oxidant effect and are considered important neutralizers of free radicals. A few studies of the role of vitamin E in protecting against breast cancer have produced contradictory results. You get vitamin E from eggs, whole-grain cereals, and vegetable oils. Fruits (black currants, grapefruit and grapefruit juice, mangoes, oranges and orange juice, strawberries, and watermelon) and vegetables (asparagus, broccoli, brussels sprouts, cauliflower, lettuce, mustard greens, parsley, green peppers, spinach, and tomato) are your best sources of vitamin C.

Cruciferous Vegetables

A number of studies have shown that cancer rates are lowest among people who consume a lot of cruciferous vegetables—cabbage, broccoli, brussels sprouts, kohlrabi, and cauliflower. And, in 1992, researchers at Johns Hopkins University School of Medicine isolated a chemical, sulforaphane, in broccoli that protects against cancer by triggering the action of tumor-fighting enzymes.

Other Threats?

There is no good evidence that other elements of the Western diet—food additives, coffee, cholesterol, or artificial sweeteners—play a role in developing cancer. In fact, some preservatives actually may protect against cancer! However, researchers are looking into recent findings suggesting that broiling or frying meat and fish may set in motion a process that has led to cancer in laboratory animals.

Other than an exceptionally strong family history, a high-fat diet seems to be the most significant risk factor for breast and ovarian cancer. As you now know, there is no *guarantee* that cutting down on fat will reduce your risks. But it may. And increasing your consumption of foods containing beta carotene and vitamins A, C, and E may help, too. What else can you do? In addition to the topics covered in this chapter, here, for the record, are the American Cancer Society's recommendations:

- Avoid obesity. (Remember, overweight women are at higher risk for both breast and ovarian cancer.)
- Cut down on total fat intake. (This you know.)
- Eat more high-fiber foods, such as whole-grain cereals, fruits, and vegetables (the staples of a low-fat diet).
- Include foods rich in vitamins A and C in your daily diet.
- Include cruciferous vegetables, such as cabbage, broc-

coli, brussels sprouts, kohlrabi, and cauliflower, in your
diet.

- Be moderate in your consumption of alcoholic beverages. (We discussed this subject in Chapter 1.)
- Be moderate in your consumption of salt-cured and ni-
trite-cured foods. (These foods have *not* been associated
with an increased risk of breast or ovarian cancer but
may play a role in stomach and esophageal cancer.)

5

Early Warning Systems

N O woman is immune to breast or ovarian cancer. All of us must remain on guard. Even women whose ovaries have been removed in the course of a hysterectomy or other surgery may not be entirely safe from ovarian cancer. And removing your breasts won't necessarily protect you from cancer if the surgery leaves behind any breast tissue.

If your risk is higher than normal, you and your doctor should step up your vigilance. For those women at very high risk, this means meticulous medical monitoring, and for women at high risk for ovarian cancer, some tests that aren't routinely recommended. Whether you need them or not is something you will have to discuss with your doctor, which brings us to the question of whether you need a specialist or can continue to rely on your family doctor or gynecologist.

FINDING THE RIGHT DOCTOR

The doctor women see most often is the gynecologist. If you are health-conscious, you probably began having annual gynecological checkups in your twenties or when you became sexually active or pregnant. All women should have an annual exam plus Pap smear until they reach 40. After that, some doctors recommend checkups every six months—although, unless an abnormality is detected, you don't need more than one Pap smear per year—because the incidence of all kinds of cancer in women increases after 40. Getting a checkup twice a year definitely makes sense if you are at higher than normal risk for either breast or ovarian cancer.

The question you may be asking yourself is whether you might be better off with a doctor who specializes or concentrates on the diagnosis and treatment of breast or ovarian cancer. The quick answer to that question is: It depends. If you don't live in or near a big city, it isn't likely that your local medical community includes a physician who treats only one disease. If you do live in a major metropolitan area, it should not be hard to find a specialist in breast diseases. Finding one who treats only ovarian cancer could be more difficult. These specialists are usually in great demand and give most of their time to patients who are sick, not to healthy women concerned about their risks. You need a good doctor who understands and appreciates your risk and concern. The stronger your family history of breast or ovarian cancer, the more urgent is your need for a doctor who stays up-to-date on the hereditary aspects of these diseases. A doctor who dismisses or minimizes your risk is probably not the physician for you. You would be better off finding a doctor who is more attuned to your level of risk and the added vigilance it demands. You don't necessarily need a specialist, but you do need a doctor who will monitor you closely.

Is your current doctor the right one for you? Do you like and trust her or him? Have you discussed your cancer risks? Better yet, has she or he noted your increased risk and suggested steps that would help detect cancer at the earliest opportunity or helped you assess your risk and put it in perspective? It is always important to have a physician with whom you can communicate.

But communication skills are no substitute for medical

expertise. You can check on a doctor's credentials in the *Directory of Medical Specialists,* available in your public library. The doctors listed are "board certified" in their medical specialty, meaning that they have taken special training, have passed rigorous qualifying exams (the specialty "boards"), and maintain certification by completing periodic continuing education courses. Doctors who are not listed are not board certified either because they have not completed any special training *or* have not taken (or passed) the certifying exam before the directory went to press.

Board certification is no guarantee that a doctor is the best physician for you, but it does provide the assurance that she or he is fully qualified to practice the specialty.

BREAST CANCER

You may have heard that most breast lumps are not cancer. That is true, but it is hard to feel optimistic when you are the one who finds the lump. Knowing something about the frequency of false alarms may help reduce the emotional—and even the financial—toll. In 1989 J. E. Devitt, M.D. of the University of Ottawa published the thought-provoking results of his study of false alarms.

He found that of 2,923 women who sought medical attention for breast problems, only 391 had cancer. Most of this group—224—discovered their lumps accidentally; another 56 found the lumps while examining their breasts. Another 94 lumps were detected by doctors in the course of routine physical exams; the 17 others were picked up on mammograms.

What about the 2,532 false alarms? Here's how the suspicious symptoms were discovered:

- Doctors detected 565 lumps during routine physical exams.
- Women found 406 in the course of breast self-examination.

- Mammograms picked up 220.
- Women found 1,341 accidentally when they felt their breasts during a bath or shower.

What are we to make of all this? It is reassuring to have such concrete evidence that so few lumps or other symptoms turn out to be cancer. The study's author argues that many of the false alarms could have been avoided if women were not encouraged to do breast self-examination under the age of 35 or to have mammograms under the age of 60. His data indicated that very few breast cancers would have been missed: in the under-35 age group, self-examination led to the discovery of only four breast cancers, all of which were so large that they probably would have soon been found accidentally. Mammography picked up only four cancers among women under 60, and of the four, one woman had had a previous breast cancer and another had had ductal carcinoma in situ (see Chapter 3). Only ten of the cancers found by routine physical examination were in women under 45, and four of the ten women had previously had breast cancer.

What all this demonstrates is that our methods of detecting breast cancer are imperfect and that the odds of missing a cancer by not following recommendations to see your doctor annually, do monthly self-exams, and have yearly mammograms after age 50 are pretty low. But they are not zero. And if you are the one who does have breast cancer instead of a harmless lump or an initially suspicious but meaningless blip on a mammogram, the risk of missing a lump is 100 percent. Most of us would rather endure a false alarm than miss a cancer.

The Doctor Is Not Always Right

Much of the time a doctor can tell by examining you whether or not a lump is suspicious. But doctors make mistakes. And when they do, patients can get hurt. Consider the results of a recent survey of successful malpractice suits: in 55 percent of all breast cancer cases, diagnosis was delayed because the doctor dismissed the importance of a lump discovered by the patient. In 35 percent of the cases, mammogram reports were negative when they should have been positive, meaning that a lump either didn't show up or was incorrectly interpreted by the physician responsible for reading the mammogram. Interestingly, 70 percent of the claims were filed by women under 50, and 40 percent by women under 40. Since breast cancer is not common under the age of 40 and is less common among women in their forties than among those past 50, chances are the physicians involved were not inclined to take seriously the lumps found among the younger women.

There is no way of knowing how often this happens. The study included 273 malpractice claims paid by 21 different insurance companies. Obviously, not every woman whose breast cancer diagnosis is delayed sues her doctor, so there may be many more of these cases than we realize.

So what should you do if your doctor dismisses a lump or other symptom that concerns you? The physician's assessment is probably correct, but it won't hurt to get a second opinion or a mammogram. Your gut feeling about what is going on in your body can be a pretty accurate barometer of reality. Further on in this chapter you will find a discussion of mammograms, their limitations, and what you should do if you feel a lump that doesn't show on the X-ray.

SELF-EXAMINATION

If you know anything at all about breast cancer detection, you know that you are supposed to examine your breasts every month looking for a lump. In a recent study at the University of Massachusetts, women with breast cancer were asked whether they did breast self-exams. Those who did examine themselves had smaller lumps at the time of diagnosis and, as a result, a much better chance of a cure;

those who didn't had bigger lumps—and therefore less optimistic outlooks.

Not only can self-examination save your life, it can save
your breast. A diagnosis of breast cancer is not a death
sentence. But recovery requires treatment, and treatment
usually means surgery. In Chapter 9 you will learn about
the surgical alternatives—lumpectomy versus mastectomy.
The general rule of thumb is that the bigger the lump, the
more potentially disfiguring the surgery will be.

Another good reason for breast self-exams is the information it gives you about your breasts; this knowledge can
save you a lot of trouble. If you can tell a physician that the
lump detected in the course of a physical exam has been
there, unchanged, for years, you can save yourself the price
of a mammogram, a biopsy, and the emotional turmoil they
engender.

What Are You Looking For?

The trouble with breast self-examination is that most
women don't know what they are looking for. Worse, they
don't know what their breasts *should* feel like—what belongs there and what doesn't. You can touch something that
feels hard, immobile, and huge—all the characteristics of
what you have heard might be cancer. Panic sets in as you
follow your fingers and then, relief—the "lump" is a rib.
This happens a lot. Honest. Then there are all those lumpy
things that slide out from under your fingers and you have
to chase around. Not to worry. That's breast tissue.

The sooner you start doing self-exams, the better ac-
quainted you will be with your breasts and the more confidence you will feel about what belongs there and what
doesn't.

This is what you are looking for: a lump (or, sometimes,
lumps) that appears suddenly (it wasn't there at your last
self-exam), stands out, and doesn't go away. Don't worry
about missing a tiny lump. It is unlikely that you will feel

anything significant that is less than one-half inch in diameter.

A few years ago, Albert R. Milan, M.D., a Baltimore obstetrician and gynecologist, described an easy way to learn the difference between a lump that may mean trouble and a harmless cyst: Close one eye and place your finger on your eyelid. Slowly move your finger so the lid slides over the surface of your eye. Then gently pluck the skin of the lid. It will lift easily. This is the way most cysts feel to the touch. Now put your finger on the tip of your nose and move it around as you did on your eyelid. Notice that you can't move the skin without moving the underlying area. You can't pluck the skin away from your nose as you did with your eye. That is what a suspicious lump feels like. Still, you should have any lump checked if it doesn't go away after one menstrual cycle.

How to Examine Your Breasts

Figure 5.1 illustrates the steps of breast self-examination. Here is what you should do and look for:

Step 1: Begin by looking at your breasts in the mirror. Do you notice anything different about them? Do your nipples look the way they always have? Is one inverted—does it turn inward instead of sticking out? If it has always been that way, fine. Check for other types of asymmetry—a dimpling or puckering of the skin that wasn't there before.

Step 2: Do this in the shower; the water reduces friction between fingers and breasts, heightening the sensitivity of the exam. Feel your breasts with the pads of the middle three fingers of the hand you are using. Press gently but firmly enough to feel breast tissue. There are three techniques you can use: (1) *circular* feeling from the outside of your breast near the armpit, around the outer edge, then move your fingers in and feel all the way around the breast again and then again until you reach the nipple; (2) *vertical strip,* feeling up and down the breast starting at the inside (closest to the opposite breast) and working your way out; and (3) *wedge,* feeling from the nipple out to the outer edge of each breast and then back in again to the nipple. (Figure 5.2 illustrates these techniques.) Repeat the technique you have chosen until you have checked the entire breast. Then switch to the opposite breast. Also feel your underarms for any swellings and make sure nothing unusual can be felt between your breasts and your neck.

Step 3: Squeeze each nipple *very gently* looking for a discharge. This is rarely a sign of cancer, and when it is, the discharge is noticeable without the squeezing.

Step 4: Repeat Steps 2 and 3 while lying down. Place the hand on the side of your body you are examining behind your head.

How Often?

Examine your breasts once a month. If you are premenopausal, wait until a week after your period. By then, any premenstrual lumpiness will have disappeared, giving you a better feel for the true condition of your breasts. If you are postmenopausal, timing doesn't matter unless you are taking estrogen, in which case you should do the exam when you finish your monthly supply of hormones. Otherwise, just choose a day—the first of the month, the fifteenth, the last of the month, any one will do.

Your Doctor's Exam

If you are seeing a gynecologist regularly, all of your routine checkups should include a breast examination. (Obviously, you don't need a breast exam every time you see your doctor for treatment unrelated to your breasts.) In general, women between 20 and 40 should have a breast exam every two or three years. Those at high risk should see a doctor annually. And all women should have more frequent exams as they get older—this means at least once a year for those women past 40 who have no increased risk

Figure 5.1. One Method of Breast Self-Examination
(*Source: National Cancer Institute*)

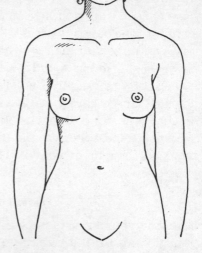

1 **(a)** Stand before a mirror. Check both breasts for anything unusual. Look for a discharge from the nipples, puckering, dimpling, or scaling of the skin.

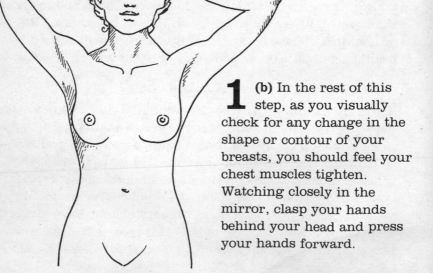

1 **(b)** In the rest of this step, as you visually check for any change in the shape or contour of your breasts, you should feel your chest muscles tighten. Watching closely in the mirror, clasp your hands behind your head and press your hands forward.

1 (c) Next, press your hands firmly on your hips and bow slightly toward the mirror as you pull your shoulders and elbows forward.

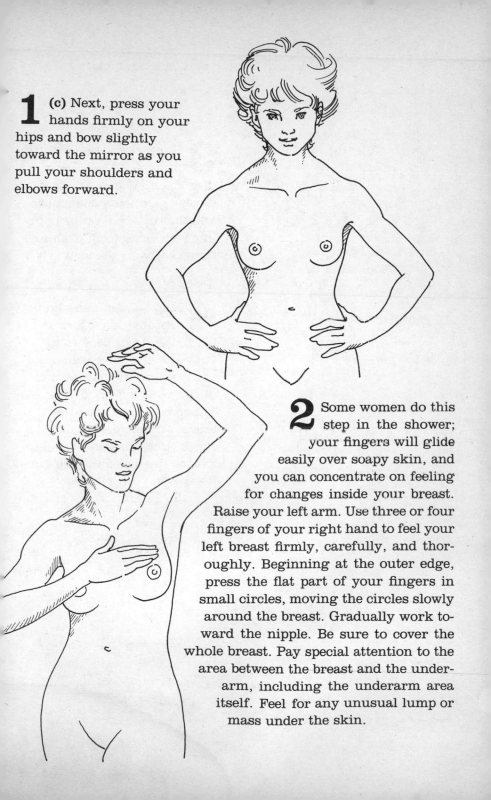

2 Some women do this step in the shower; your fingers will glide easily over soapy skin, and you can concentrate on feeling for changes inside your breast. Raise your left arm. Use three or four fingers of your right hand to feel your left breast firmly, carefully, and thoroughly. Beginning at the outer edge, press the flat part of your fingers in small circles, moving the circles slowly around the breast. Gradually work toward the nipple. Be sure to cover the whole breast. Pay special attention to the area between the breast and the underarm, including the underarm area itself. Feel for any unusual lump or mass under the skin.

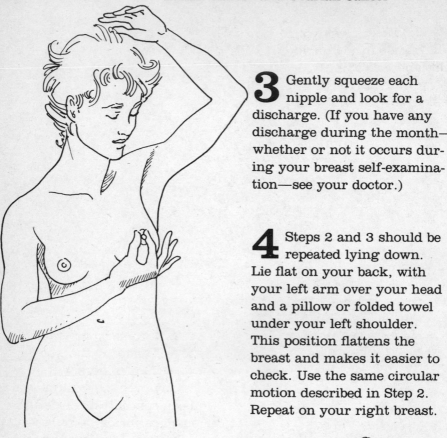

3 Gently squeeze each nipple and look for a discharge. (If you have any discharge during the month—whether or not it occurs during your breast self-examination—see your doctor.)

4 Steps 2 and 3 should be repeated lying down. Lie flat on your back, with your left arm over your head and a pillow or folded towel under your left shoulder. This position flattens the breast and makes it easier to check. Use the same circular motion described in Step 2. Repeat on your right breast.

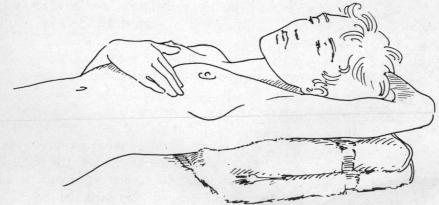

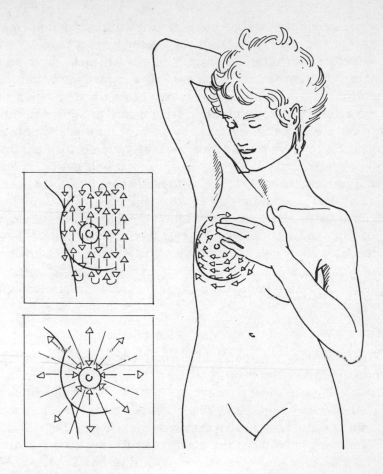

Figure 5.2 Alternative Method of Breast Self-
Examination: (*Source: American Cancer Society. Used
with permission.*)

of breast cancer. Women past 40 with a higher than normal risk should consider seeing the doctor twice a year.

Doctors can often distinguish between suspicious and harmless lumps, and some can take immediate action to determine whether a lump is a cyst (see the discussion of cysts in Chapter 3). Not all physicians are proficient in this procedure. For this reason, your doctor may send you to a surgeon to have a cyst aspirated. If your doctor has any doubts about the nature of a lump, you will need a mammogram and possibly a biopsy to make sure it is not cancer.

Physical examination is particularly important for women with small breasts. Mammography is less efficient for "flat-chested" women simply because they have less breast to compress between the X-ray plates. Conversely, mammograms are more useful than physical exams in spotting suspicious changes in large breasts—the doctor can examine only areas close to the surface of the breast.

MAMMOGRAMS

These breast X-rays can pick up cancers too small to be felt by a woman or her doctor, tumors as tiny as one-fifth of an inch. (You can't feel a tumor until it grows to two-fifths of an inch.) Although early detection can save lives, it is far from certain how much mammograms really help. Still, mammograms can be immensely reassuring—they can distinguish between harmless cysts or fibroadenomas (see Chapter 3) and suspicious lumps. For this reason, they serve as a valuable diagnostic tool. But controversy abounds about the value of using mammograms to screen women with no symptoms of breast cancer.

Limitations

For all their much-touted benefits, mammograms do have their limitations. In the first place, they are not particularly good at picking up breast cancer in young women. Young breasts are "dense"—they have more breast tissue than fat.

Since tumors are the same density as breast tissue, they won't show up when nestled in breast tissue. They do show up clearly when situated in fatty (not dense) areas of the breast.

Doctors generally do not recommend screening mammograms for women under 35, for two reasons. First of all, breast cancer rarely occurs in this age group, and second, even when it does, the dense tissue of young breasts can obscure a tumor. This picture changes with age: the risk of breast cancer begins to increase at 40 and rises even faster after 50. Over those same years the composition of the breast also changes: breast tissue gradually yields to fat. As a result, tumors in older women show up more readily on mammograms.

In addition, mammograms do not give a complete picture of the breast. You have breast tissue all the way up to your armpit and extending up your chest wall toward your collarbone. The part of the breast that the mammography machine's compression device can capture is only the area that sticks out most prominently from the body.

Effectiveness

The rationale for having regular mammograms is that picking up cancers two years before they are big enough to be felt as a lump in the breast saves lives. Early evidence from a clinical trial conducted in the 1960s by the Health Insurance Plan (HIP) of Greater New York Screening Program indicated that 10 years after their cancer had been diagnosed, the death rate among women over 50 whose tumors had been detected by mammography was 30 percent lower than that of women whose cancer was not found until a lump appeared. Initially, the same study found no survival advantage among women under 50 whose cancers had been found by mammography. However, follow-up data published in 1986 showed a slight advantage: only 36 women who were under 50 when their cancer was found via mammography have died, compared with 42 among those in the same-size comparison group who discovered their cancer when a lump appeared.

Why doesn't early detection save more lives? In Chapter 3 you read that by the time breast cancer is discovered on a mammogram it has been around for six to eight years— plenty of time for cancer cells to break off from the tumor and move elsewhere in the body. Still, chances are that breast cancer detected via mammography will not have spread. About 90 percent of women whose tumors are tiny and who show no evidence that cancer has spread to their lymph nodes are alive and well 10 years later.

Risks

The mammography risk that seems to concern women most is the danger of radiation exposure. Although the amount of radiation per mammogram is extremely small, it does have a cumulative effect. The odds of developing breast cancer as a result of this exposure are minimal, but they are not zero. It has been estimated that out of 25,000 women between the ages of 40 and 49 who have mammograms annually for 10 years, one will develop radiation-induced breast cancer. The rate is lower among older women—about one case per 50,000—because their breasts are not as dense. The denser the breast tissue, the greater the effect of the radiation.

Unfortunately, mammograms are also not error-proof. Even mammograms done at the best facilities by the best-trained technicians and interpreted by the most experienced radiologists can be wrong: about 10 percent of all breast cancer doesn't show up on mammograms, for several reasons:

- It was in an area that couldn't be seen on the X-ray.
- It was hidden by dense breast tissue.
- It didn't look suspicious to the radiologist.

The error or "false negative" rate can be much higher than 10 percent when facilities and personnel aren't top-notch.

Although mammograms can save lives, a false negative result can be costly to the woman who loses the early detection advantage. And errors can also take a huge financial and emotional toll. A false positive mammogram suggesting that cancer is present can lead to a biopsy and engender a lot of heartache and worry. In this country nine out of every ten biopsies performed to investigate suspicious mammographic findings are negative—the women do not have cancer.

So Why Have Mammograms?

Despite the risks and limitations of mammograms, there are two compelling reasons to have them: They may save your life, and they can save your breast. When a tiny tumor is detected, it has to be removed. The two surgical options are mastectomy, the removal of the breast, and lumpectomy, the removal of the malignant lump and some surrounding tissue where cancer cells may lurk. In general, the smaller the lump when cancer is detected, the less disfiguring the surgery required. You will find more information about both mastectomy and lumpectomy in Chapter 9.

Who Should Have Mammograms?

Obviously, you should have a mammogram if you develop a lump in your breast that your physician regards as suspicious. (A mammogram can reassure you that the lump is not cancer. However, if the results are not definitive, a biopsy may be needed. And if you feel a lump that does not show up on a mammogram, you may need a biopsy to find out whether the lump is benign or malignant.)

The American Cancer Society, the National Cancer Institute, the American Medical Association, and nine other organizations concerned with cancer detection have agreed on the following recommendations for screening for cancer in women who have no symptoms:

- Women over 40 should have their breasts examined by a physician at least once a year and a mammogram every one to two years.
- Women over 50 should have a breast examination and a mammogram every year.

You may need a follow-up mammogram six months after your first one if any abnormality is seen. This happens a lot—every woman's breasts are different. Although experienced radiologists usually can tell the difference between what could be malignant and what is not, caution dictates a second look six months later. If there is no change, you can be certain that whatever showed up is just normal for your breasts. There is no point in doing the follow-up before six months elapse because in the unlikely event that the abnormality is cancer, no detectable change will show up in a shorter period of time.

Where to Go

It does make a difference where you have your mammograms. To reduce the risk of a false positive or false negative finding, and to be certain that you are getting the lowest possible dose of radiation, you should do a little shopping around before deciding where to go. The best mammograms are done on X-ray machines designed especially for this purpose. Both the technicians who take the mammograms and the physicians who read them should have special training and perform mammograms regularly.

The American College of Radiology (ACR) has established standards for performing mammography and awards a certificate to radiology facilities that meet those standards. However, since the certification program is voluntary, there is no reason to assume that an uncertified center does not maintain very high standards. However, ACR certification can save you the trouble of checking out mammography centers in your area. You can get a list of certified centers in your state by writing or calling the ACR. (See Appendix 5 for the address and phone number.)

You can assess a mammography center for yourself by asking the following questions:

- Is the radiologist who reads the mammogram certified by the American Board of Radiology or the American Osteopathy Board of Radiology?
- If the radiologist is not board-certified, has he or she had at least two months of full-time training in mammography interpretation, medical radiation physics, radiation effects, and radiation protection?
- How many mammograms does the radiologist interpret or review per year? (The correct answer here should be at least 480.)
- Is the technician certified by the American Registry of Radiological Technologists and/or licensed by the state?
- Does he or she perform mammograms regularly?
- Is the equipment designed especially for mammography?
- Does the equipment have a removable grid? A grid is a device needed to enhance X-ray contrast of dense breasts. The radiation dose is slightly higher when a grid is used. It should be used only when the technician is X-raying a dense breast and removed from the equipment when he or she is X-raying women whose breasts are not dense.
- How often is the equipment calibrated? To ensure that the radiation dose emitted is no more than 0.4 rad per exposure, the equipment should be tested and calibrated at least once a year.

Does It Hurt?

To get a good picture, the technician will have to squeeze your breast between two flat plates on the mammography machine. This compression is necessary and may be momentarily uncomfortable. But it lasts only for the very short time it takes the technician to complete positioning you and to retreat behind the machine to snap the picture—a matter of seconds. Some breasts are more sensitive than others, so you could experience some brief discomfort. Most women don't seem to mind and say it wouldn't stop them from having mammograms in the future. If you are premenopausal and experience premenstrual breast tenderness, it is a good idea to schedule your mammograms for the week after your period ends in order to avoid or decrease discomfort.

When Do You Get the Results?

Sometimes you'll get the results right away. When a radiologist is on the scene, he or she will look at the mammogram immediately to make sure that the picture turned out and to see what it shows. Some radiologists may tell you right away that everything is fine. Sometimes the doctor will ask the technician to take another view of the breast to get a clearer or bigger picture of something that didn't show up to best advantage on the first picture. This "something" is usually not cancer, so don't panic if the doctor orders another view.

If something suspicious does show up, the radiologist may suggest an ultrasound exam, which may show whether a lump is solid or a cyst. In some centers, this can be done on the spot.

When a radiologist isn't available, you will have to wait a few days for the results. If your doctor referred you to the center, the results will go to his or her office, where you will have to telephone. Bad news travels fast—if there is something to worry about, you probably will hear from your physician before you make the call.

If you have your mammograms done in a mobile van or a center where only mammograms are performed, your results usually will be mailed to you. These high-volume facilities can provide mammograms at low cost because they are staffed by technicians. At the end of the day, all the mammograms go to radiologists who interpret them and write the reports. The advantage of these centers is that their costs are generally much lower than elsewhere. The disadvantage is that, to keep costs down, they have no doctor on hand to look at the mammograms right away and talk to you about the findings. Many of these facilities maintain very high standards. But as with any mammography site, check them out first.

ULTRASOUND

This painless detection method sends high-frequency sound waves through the breast to create a black-and-white television image from which a doctor can determine whether a lump is a cyst or a solid lump. The sound waves will pass right through cysts but bounce off solid lumps. Ultrasound won't tell you, however, whether a lump is benign, malignant, or premalignant. Because it cannot pick up very small lumps, ultrasound is not an efficient method of screening women for breast cancer. However, ultrasound can save a lot of diagnostic time and trouble by distinguishing between cysts and lumps seen on mammograms.

BIOPSY

A biopsy is a surgical procedure to remove tissue for study under a microscope to see if cancer is present. There are four kinds of breast biopsies. In Chapter 3 we discussed aspirating a lump to make sure it is a fluid-filled cyst. This procedure is a type of biopsy even though, in most cases, the fluid removed goes down the drain, not to the lab. Another similar type of biopsy, fine-needle aspiration, involves using a needle to remove some cells from a solid lump for laboratory studies. Both of these aspirating procedures usually can be performed in the doctor's office.

The other two types of biopsies are surgical procedures to remove all or part of a suspicious lump. Excisional biopsy removes the entire lump; incisional biopsy takes only a piece of the lump. Most surgeons prefer to do excisional biopsies whenever possible. In effect, these are lumpectomies because the entire lump plus some surrounding tissue is removed. The big advantage of excisional biopsy is that if the lump is malignant, you get diagnosis (the biopsy) and treatment at the same time. You will need more surgery if you opt for a mastectomy. (See Chapter 9 for a discussion of mastectomy versus lumpectomy.)

These days incisional biopsies are done only when the lump is so large that removing all of it would involve extensive surgery requiring a general anesthetic. Most biopsies of either type are done with a local anesthetic.

What's Involved

Biopsies today are usually outpatient procedures—you enter and leave the hospital the same day. As noted above, you probably will be given local anesthesia, which numbs only the area of your breast over the lump. You may be given a tranquilizer first—that is up to your doctor, and you should discuss the subject in advance. The anesthesia takes effect immediately. You won't feel the incision itself, but you will feel some pulling and pressure.

The anesthesia wears off about an hour after the incision is sewn up and bandaged. There may be some soreness for a few days. Many women feel better wearing a bra, even during the night, until the soreness disappears. You usually can resume normal activities and shower the day after the biopsy.

It takes about a week for the incision to heal. If your stitches are under the skin, you don't have to go back to the doctor to have them removed. If not, you'll have to see the surgeon about a week after the biopsy to have your stitches taken out.

When Do You Get the Results?

You may get preliminary results of the biopsy before you leave the hospital. As soon as the lump is removed it goes to the pathologist, who slices off a section, quick-freezes it, stains it, and examines it under a microscope. The results of this "frozen section" are not always the last word on the subject. A more reliable "permanent section" will be prepared from remaining parts of the lump. Because several steps are involved, the permanent section may not go under the microscope for 24–36 hours. The pathologist examines it, makes a diagnosis, and writes a report for the surgeon. All of this takes time, which explains why you may have to wait as long as a week for the results.

OVARIAN CANCER

There are no early symptoms of ovarian cancer (see Chapter 6), making it very difficult to find before it spreads. Researchers are looking for "markers"—chemical changes that show up in the blood that would help doctors spot the disease at the earliest possible opportunity. Today ovarian cancer is found early only by accident when the ovaries are examined during surgery for conditions affecting other pelvic organs. Ovarian cancer is usually discovered either after symptoms develop or when abnormalities are found during regular gynecologic checkups.

Some doctors now recommend that women with a strong family history of ovarian cancer have biannual checkups that include a pelvic exam and an ultrasound examination of the ovaries.

PELVIC EXAMS

During a routine pelvic examination, a doctor often can feel irregular ovarian growths that could mean cancer. These are particularly significant when they are found in post-menopausal women. After menopause the ovaries shrink until they are no longer palpable (can no longer be felt) during a pelvic exam. An ovary that is palpable in a post-menopausal woman is cause for concern and always should be followed up with a biopsy to rule out ovarian cancer. Ovarian enlargements in younger women are somewhat less worrisome since they are much more likely to be harmless cysts than malignant tumors (see Chapter 3). Still, these growths always should be investigated surgic-ally if they don't disappear after two or three menstrual cycles.

ULTRASOUND

When a suspicious ovarian growth is detected during a pelvic exam, the first order of business is often an ultra-sound examination, which can detect ovarian growths and distinguish between cysts and solid tumors. (See discus-sion of ultrasound in the breast cancer section of this chapter.)

CA-125

The search for markers that could indicate the presence of a malignant ovarian tumor before symptoms develop or growths can be detected in the course of a pelvic exam has zeroed in on CA-125, an antibody produced by epithelial cancer cells (see Chapter 3). The blood test for CA-125—which, theoretically, helps doctors distinguish between women with early ovarian cancer and those who are disease-free—has so far not proved particularly useful. It produces too many false positive results, erroneously suggesting that cancer is present when in fact none exists. The high false positive rate probably stems from the fact that CA-125 levels can rise in response to normal menstruation, endometriosis, ectopic pregnancy, and a number of other gynecologic conditions as well as ovarian cancer. For the present, the CA-125 test is proving most useful in monitoring treatment response and relapse rates among women who have ovarian cancer. (When treatment is successful, CA-125 levels should fall to normal; if they rise after treatment, the cancer may have recurred.)

OTHER MARKERS

Several other blood markers of ovarian cancer have been identified, although so far none has proved helpful in initial diagnosis.

Carcinoembryonic Antigen (CEA): Increased levels of this protein are sometimes found in women with ovarian cancer. However, higher than normal CEA levels also have been seen in people who smoke cigarettes as well as among patients with other kinds of cancer, benign tumors, inflammatory disorders, liver disease, and lung infections. For an elevated CEA to be a meaningful indication of ovarian cancer, doctors would have to ascertain that their patients do not smoke and that they don't have any of the other conditions associated with an elevated CEA. However, monitoring CEA levels can help determine whether treatment for ovarian cancer is working or if a recurrence is under way.

Alpha-fetoprotein (AFP): Levels of this blood protein tend to rise when one particular type of ovarian tumor, the endodermal sinus tumor, is present but can also be elevated in patients with several kinds of liver disease. Increasing AFP levels can help doctors diagnose rapidly enlarging solid ovarian growths as endodermal sinus tumors.

Human Chorionic Gonadotropin (HCG): Elevated levels of

this hormone are sometimes found among women with germ cell tumors (see Chapter 3). Like the other markers for ovarian cancer, this one is useful only as an aid in monitoring the effectiveness of treatment. It is not specific enough to help with detection of ovarian cancer.

TRANSVAGINAL ULTRASOUND

This promising new method of detecting ovarian cancer was developed in England. It uses a vaginal probe to conduct an ultrasound scan of the ovaries. Transvaginal ultrasound is much more specific than conventional ultrasound because it defines the ovary more accurately in order to detect suspicious abnormalities. Studies are now under way to further assess the usefulness of transvaginal ultrasound as a screening technique. On the basis of their findings, the British researchers concluded that transvaginal ultrasound screening every 12–18 months would be necessary to catch ovarian cancer early in its development before it begins to spread. An even newer test, Transvaginal Doppler Color Flow Imaging, can spot abnormal blood flow to the ovaries. This may indicate a developing growth although it cannot distinguish between benign and malignant tumors.

SURGERY

Today surgery is the only way to positively determine that an ovarian growth is benign or malignant. In general, the more suspicious the growth, the more extensive the surgery recommended to investigate its nature. Enough cells for a biopsy can be obtained via laparoscopy—surgery conducted with the aid of a laparascope, a long thin tube with a tiny telescope through which the surgeon can see internal structures and extract the tissue needed for biopsy. Laparoscopy sometimes can be performed on an outpatient basis. If no cancer is found, the patient can go home the same day with no more than a small bandage over the tiny incision through which the laparascope was inserted. If cancer is found, further surgery will be needed (see Chapter 9).

The surgical alternative to laparascopy is a procedure called laparotomy, which is done through a much larger abdominal incision. This allows the surgeon to remove the suspicious growth and, if it proves to be malignant, to explore the abdominal cavity to see whether or not the cancer has spread and to remove affected organs (see Chapter 9). Laparotomy requires a hospital stay of five to seven days or longer depending on the extent of surgery.

CHAPTER

6

Signs and Symptoms

THE trouble with both breast and ovarian cancer is that neither can be detected early. As you learned in Chapter 3, even the tiniest breast lumps found by mammograms have been growing for six to eight years before they can be seen on the X-rays. Luckily, most of these tiny cancers have not spread beyond the breast and are indeed early breast cancers that usually can be cured. But until a lump develops that can be detected by mammography or felt by a woman or her doctor, breast cancer rarely produes symptoms: no pain and no obvious changes signifying something is wrong.

Ovarian cancer presents even more of a diagnostic problem since there is no reliable way to examine the ovaries for signs of impending cancer. In fact, researchers know very little about the physical changes leading up to this disease. Despite these disadvantages, alert women may notice vague symptoms that could help doctors detect ovarian cancer before it becomes more obvious. We will review the signs and symptoms of breast and ovarian cancer in this chapter and will also discuss the ultimate in prevention: surgery to remove the breasts or ovaries.

BREAST CANCER

In Chapter 5 you learned how to examine your breasts and what external and internal changes to look for. Here we will focus on the significance of these changes.

Lumps

In Chapter 3 we discussed the different types of lumps that can form in the breast, including harmless cysts and fibroadenomas as well as benign and malignant tumors. Any lump that does not shrink or disappear after one or two menstrual cycles should be investigated. If you faithfully examine your breasts every month, you usually can tell the difference between a new "dominant" lump and those that have been there before. The sooner you see your doctor to check out a new lump, the sooner you will allay your anxiety about what it is. Most are not cancer, but there is no way to tell for sure without a medical evaluation that includes a physical exam by your doctor, a mammogram if suggested, an ultrasound examination if the mammogram provides no definitive answers, and if these tests aren't conclusive, a biopsy to determine the nature of the lump.

Skin Changes

Sometimes changes in the surface of the skin foretell cancer. Usually these changes are not apparent until the cancer is advanced, but they should never be ignored. Among them:

Swelling: This can happen with advanced cancer, a tumor more than two inches large. How can a lump get so big without being noticed? Usually it cannot. The woman with this advanced a cancer has often known about the lump for a long time but has been too frightened to see a doctor. The outlook here is not always as bleak as you might imagine. A tumor that has been around for a long time without causing disease elsewhere in the body probably is not growing very fast. On the other hand, some very aggressive cancers may seem to appear overnight, bringing with them a lump plus external skin symptoms.

Ulcerating Skin: This can also happen with the advanced cancer described above.

Skin Redness: This may be a sign of infection or a symptom of inflammatory breast cancer. The skin is warm as well as red and may feel thick or hard. Sometimes, the affected area is painful. These cancers can be mistaken for infections because (1) infections are common and inflammatory breast cancer is rare, and (2) there may be no lump underlying the reddened area. The redness develops because cancer cells are blocking normal drainage of fluid from the skin via the lymphatic vessels.

Enlarged Lymph Nodes

Occasionally, breast cancer is discovered because a woman notices swollen lymph nodes in her underarm area. A biopsy shows breast cancer cells, but no lump can be felt. A mammogram usually will reveal a small tumor, but occasionally nothing shows up. This means that the tumor is still very, very small but obviously big enough for cancer cells to peel off and travel elsewhere, the first stop being the affected lymph nodes. When no sign of cancer can be found on a mammogram, treatment becomes problematical. How does a surgeon remove a lump that can't be found? Alternatives include mastectomy, which has one big advantage: You will get rid of the cancer in the breast. But since you already have evidence that cancer cells have migrated beyond the breast, mastectomy seems a bit extreme. If the lump could be located, lumpectomy would be all the surgery the woman would need. (See Chapter 9 for a discussion of lumpectomy versus mastectomy.) Radiation therapy might kill off the cancer cells in the breast, but this kind of treatment is most efficient when targeted at a specific site. It makes much more sense to use chemotherapy, drugs that can kill off microscopic clusters of cancer cells. Chemotherapy usually is recommended when lymph nodes are positive in women who do have tumors, so it also makes sense to use the drugs when nodes are positive and there is no (detectable) lump.

Another option is to remove the upper, outer quarter of the breast, where most cancers occur. You can see what a dilemma these cases pose; luckily, they are rare.

OVARIAN CANCER

The earliest symptom of ovarian cancer is abdominal swelling, an indication that the disease already is advanced. This swelling is due to the accumulation of fluid called ascites in the abdomen.

However, months before this dramatic symptom occurs, some women complain of vague digestive symptoms: indigestion, gassiness, nausea, feeling full after eating a light meal, a slight loss of appetite.

Unfortunately, the digestive disturbances linked to ovarian cancer are very common in our society and become more common with age. Americans spend millions of dollars every year on antigas medications. Bothersome as these digestive symptoms can be, most people don't take them very seriously and rightly so—they usually are not medically significant. Indeed, these complaints are so common and, for the most part, so medically meaningless that most doctors do not take them seriously either. The most common prescription is a bit of reassurance and a recommendation to take one of the many over-the-counter remedies available.

However, persistent digestive complaints in a woman over 40 could be a sign of ovarian cancer and should never be ignored, either by the patient or her doctor. If an explanation cannot be found, women with these symptoms definitely should be evaluated for ovarian cancer.

Other telltale symptoms can include vaginal bleeding in postmenopausal women and, as described in Chapter 5, a normal-sized or enlarged ovary in a woman past menopause.

Ovarian cancer rarely causes menstrual irregularities in premenopausal women.

DRASTIC MEASURES

Given that ovarian cancer is usually advanced by the time symptoms occur, and that even breast cancer detected "early" via mammograms may have spread beyond the breast, the only way to entirely eliminate the threat to life these diseases pose is surgical removal of the breast or ovaries. We touched on this subject in Chapter 2. Here we will examine these procedures in more detail.

PROPHYLACTIC MASTECTOMY

Removing the breast to prevent breast cancer is called prophylactic mastectomy. Why would a woman want to remove a healthy breast? And why would a doctor cooperate?

Obviously, this type of surgery is never likely to become routine, even among women whose risk is higher than normal. However, it might be a sensible course of action for very high-risk women from hereditary breast cancer families (see Chapter 2). These women are in great danger: chances can be as high as 50–50 that they have inherited the defective gene responsible for the many cases of breast cancer in their families. In Chapter 7 you will read the personal stories of women who fall into this very high-risk category.

How high does a woman's risk of breast cancer have to be before she considers prophylactic mastectomy? Most doctors would agree that it should be pretty high. A woman whose chances of *not* developing breast cancer are substantially higher than her chances of developing it would not, under normal circumstances, be a candidate. Of course, there are some women who are "cancer-phobic"; they fear the disease so much that they simply cannot live with any additional degree of risk. They might be better off in counseling or psychotherapy to help them deal with their fears and put their risk in proper perspective, but a determined woman can always find a cooperative surgeon. Unfortunately, no widely accepted medical guidelines exist for doctors to follow in deciding on their patients' candidacy for prophylactic mastectomy. Indeed, some doctors might actually frighten a woman into the surgery by emphasizing the extent of her risk. Many doctors will refuse to perform this very controversial operation except on women whose risk is demonstrably very high. What's more, your health insurance policy may not cover prophylactic mastectomy, even when you are at extremely high risk for breast cancer.

The Surgery

There are two types of prophylactic mastectomy. One, subcutaneous mastectomy, involves removing the breast tissue and fat via a small incision. The surgeon then replaces the tissue with a saline-filled implant. The visible part of the breast is left intact: the nipple and areola and skin remain. Only the inside is replaced.

Appealing as this operation may sound, it has its drawbacks. A surgeon following this procedure cannot remove all of the breast tissue. Some will be left that could provide fertile ground for breast cancer, so that you will have had drastic surgery that has not completely eliminated your risk.

A more reasonable alternative is to remove both breasts and do immediate reconstruction. All the normal breast tissue is gone for good, leaving no chance that cancer will occur. The breast may look natural from the outside, but on the inside it is no longer a breast. If you are looking for a guarantee, this is the surgery that will give it to you.

PROPHYLACTIC OOPHORECTOMY

Every year hundreds of thousands of women have their ovaries removed regardless of their personal risk of ovarian cancer. Oophorectomy is often routine for women over 40 who are having hysterectomies for other gynecologic problems. However, removing healthy ovaries has become increasingly controversial in recent years. Some doctors now argue passionately against routine oophorectomies. Others argue just as passionately in favor of them as the only way to prevent ovarian cancer. Both sides have legitimate and persuasive points of view.

Since ovarian cancer cannot be detected before it is advanced, it would seem to make sense to protect women when the opportunity arises. You can't get ovarian cancer if you don't have ovaries. (Or at least, most women can't—see Chapter 2 for a discussion of a very rare type of ovarian cancer that occurs in women whose ovaries have been removed.) Proponents of routine prophylactic oophorectomy argue that when a woman passes 40, her ovaries gradually cease functioning. After menopause, they begin to shrink until they can no longer be palpated (felt) by a doctor in the course of a pelvic examination. However, this is also the age at which the incidence of ovarian cancer begins to rise. The apparently useless ovaries are still capable of giving rise to cancer. Incidence of the disease peaks among women around age 60, but cases continue to occur even among women in their eighties.

The other side of the argument is equally powerful. Its chief proponent is Celso-Ramon Garcia, M.D., director of infertility surgery at the Hospital of the University of Pennsylvania. He argues that the rate of ovarian cancer among women whose ovaries have been retained at hysterectomy is extremely low, only 0.01 percent, and does not justify depriving hundreds of thousands of women of their ovaries every year. Dr. Garcia contends that even aging ovaries continue to secrete hormones that may help protect women against osteoporosis, the bone thinning that accelerates after menopause and leads to millions of hip fractures and deaths among elderly women. He disputes doctors who argue that estrogen replacement can compensate women hormonally for the loss of their ovaries and maintains that the amounts currently prescribed won't bring levels back to normal.

Removing the ovaries plunges premenopausal women into instant menopause, complete with hot flashes and other symptoms that often are more severe than they would have been if menopause had arrived as a result of a gradual slowdown in ovarian function. Many women who have had their ovaries removed at hysterectomy complain of a variety of symptoms ranging from joint and bone pain to a lack of sexual desire. Since the ovaries secrete small amounts of androgen, the hormone responsible for both male and female libido, their removal may be related to this latter problem. Our current knowledge about the role the maturing ovaries play in maintaining libido is "primitive at best," says Dr. Garcia.

Some doctors may advise removing the ovaries in all women over 40; others may make this recommendation only for women who are past 45 or 50. There are no hard-and-fast medical guidelines here.

So what is a woman to decide?

Clearly, her decision depends on how she and her doctor evaluate her risk of ovarian cancer. A woman with no known risk factors may feel perfectly comfortable in retaining her ovaries at hysterectomy regardless of her age. Most doctors do not recommend routinely removing the ovaries in women under 40 at normal risk for ovarian cancer, although some may suggest it if a woman has had all the children she wants. Women with a family history of the disease—like Carol, whose story we told in Chapter 2— probably would feel safer without their ovaries. And women with a strong family history of ovarian cancer may be advised to have prophylactic oophorectomies regardless of any other medical need for hysterectomy.

The Surgery

Prophylactic oophorectomy usually is performed in the context of a hysterectomy during which the uterus, cervix, and fallopian tubes are also removed. Most hysterectomies require an abdominal incision that can be a so-called Pfannenstiel, or bikini-line, cut just above the pubic hairline rather than the less cosmetically desirable vertical incision. (Sometimes the uterus can be removed through the vagina; this procedure does not require an abdominal incision. The ovaries and fallopian tubes remain in place.) Women usually spend five to seven days in the hospital and need another six weeks to recuperate fully at home. Estrogen replacement therapy to compensate a premenopausal woman for the hormones her ovaries produced typically begins before she leaves the hospital.

CHAPTER

7

Facing Up to Your Risks

W^E all have very personal ways of living with risk. The fact that you have chosen to read this book indicates that you are taking a positive approach to it. You want to take control of your life and not wait passively wondering whether cancer will strike. We can all learn something about facing up to risk—and receive encouragement—from women who have confronted truly terrifying odds and done something to change them. In this chapter we present the case histories of four remarkable women. No matter what your risk—normal, slightly elevated, or significantly above average—we think you will find the stories that follow inspiring. All of the women faced the highest risk cancer can present. They are all from families with very strong family histories of breast or ovarian cancer or both. The path these courageous women have chosen is certainly not for everyone, but their determination to beat the odds holds lessons for us all.

CAROLYN R.

Carolyn was only three years old when her mother, then 32, developed breast cancer. "First it was in her right breast," says Carolyn, "and 18 months later it showed up in her left breast. Then she developed ovarian cancer." Carolyn's mother died at the age of 39, leaving four young daughters. Initially, Carolyn and her family believed her mother's breast cancer had spread to her ovaries. But eventually they learned that both diseases had been primary and that their mother suffered from the rare breast-ovarian cancer syndrome. Other relatives had had breast cancer, too; an aunt was diagnosed at age 38, and Carolyn's grandmother developed the disease when she was 76.

When Carolyn and her sisters began to approach the age at which their mother's breast cancer had been diagnosed, their stepmother suggested that they begin having mammograms. Their doctors agreed, and all four went for the breast X-rays. "All our mammograms were normal except for my oldest sister's," recalls Carolyn. "There was a lump in her right breast that the radiologist thought was a fibroadenoma [a benign growth—see Chapter 3]. My sister decided to have it taken out. At first things looked fine—there was no sign of cancer. But further studies of tissue from the lump showed a malignancy. My sister had a modified radical mastectomy of her right breast [removal of the breast, underarm lymph nodes, and lining over the chest muscles]. Because of our family history, she decided to have her left breast removed via a simple mastectomy [removal of the breast]."

Although Carolyn's mammogram had been normal, she felt a hard lump "the size of a pea" in her left breast. "I couldn't get my mind off of it," she recalls. "One day at the office a coworker's husband walked in and caught me with my hand under my shirt!" She asked the breast clinic to reread her mammogram and pay special attention to the area where she felt the lump. The X-ray showed nothing. Within two months the pea-sized lump had grown to the size of the first joint of Carolyn's thumb and felt "like a long piece of twisted rope." When her gynecologist felt the lump, he sent her to a surgeon for a biopsy. "I wasn't surprised to find that the lump was malignant," says Carolyn. She was 27 at the time.

The surgeon offered her the option of lumpectomy, "but I chose to do what my sister and my aunt had done. I had a modified radical mastectomy and decided to have the other breast removed with a simple mastectomy."

Carolyn's lymph nodes were negative, but "the cancer had spread from the nipple to the chest wall so I had to have seven weeks of radiation. Since then, I have had normal checkups."

In view of what looked like a very strong family history, Carolyn's other two sisters decided upon prophylactic mastectomies.

"Fear is no way to live," says Carolyn. "My sisters and I know the effect of losing a mother to cancer."

Carolyn thought she had covered all her bases until she mentioned to a nurse her fears that her young daughter's risk of breast cancer would be high, too. The nurse suggested that Carolyn contact the Hereditary Cancer Institute at Omaha's Creighton University.

The team at Creighton established that Carolyn's mother had died of ovarian cancer, not breast cancer, and traced the disease back to her maternal grandfather, whose sister had died of ovarian cancer. Her grandfather probably inherited the genetic defect responsible for his sister's cancer and passed it to Carolyn's mother, who then transmitted it to Carolyn and her oldest sister. The other two sisters might also carry the genetic trait responsible for all the breast cancer in the family. Neither was willing to wait and see.

Once they realized that they were at risk for ovarian as well as breast cancer, Carolyn and two of her three sisters had their ovaries removed. At the time the fourth sister had not yet completed her family.

"When my mother died, I thought that by the time I was old enough to get breast cancer doctors would know much more about it," says Carolyn. "Now I hope that by the time my six-year-old daughter grows up they will know what to do."

She has absolutely no regrets about the course of action she chose. "I felt I was taking charge of my body, taking charge of my life. I have done everything I could to help myself," says Carolyn. "I am going to live to see my children grow up. Period. That's it."

CLAUDIA S.

Claudia had been married just a year and a half when her mother, age 48, died of ovarian cancer. "My mother's sister died of ovarian cancer, too," says Claudia, "but when I asked my gynecologist if the disease was hereditary, he said no." That was 20 years ago. Claudia already was aware that "there was a lot of cancer in my family." Some years later she began to see newspaper and magazine articles about a local doctor, Henry T. Lynch, M.D., of Creighton's Hereditary Cancer Institute. "I decided to do a family tree to document all the cancer among my relatives," says Claudia. It took a year to get all the information together. Not long after that, Claudia's younger sister developed breast cancer. It was then that Claudia and her sisters went to see Dr. Lynch. "He told us there could be a link between ovarian cancer and breast cancer, and when he saw how much ovarian cancer there is in our family, he recommended that we all consider hysterectomies," says Claudia. Not long after that one of Claudia's first cousins developed breast cancer.

"For a while," recalls Claudia, "I was almost obsessed by the subject. I felt it was very important to do as much research as I could. I read books, magazine articles. I called the Gilda Radner Familial Ovarian Cancer Registry. I talked to gynecologic oncologists, to my personal physician. Everyone agreed that my sisters and I should have the hysterectomies."

Claudia remembers riding her exercise bike during this period and saying to herself, "I am not going to get this. I am not going to let this get me. There are some people with a family history of breast cancer who say they feel better not thinking about it. That doesn't work for me. I am a doer."

Claudia and her sisters have all had hysterectomies now. "We understand that it is not a guarantee, but having had the hysterectomies does give us some security." (Some women with strong family histories of ovarian cancer who have their ovaries removed have developed intra-abdominal carcinomatosis, a malignancy identical to ovarian cancer—see Chapter 2.)

Claudia watches herself carefully for any sign of breast cancer—she does breast self-examination faithfully every month and has an annual mammogram. She has had a gynecological checkup every six months since she was married, "because of what happened to my mother." She is also very careful about her diet: "I try not to eat too much beef, and I'm very conscious of what my kids eat."

She is also very sensitive to the fears and feelings of the young girls in the family. "When my daughter's breasts started to develop, she was afraid that what she thought was a lump was cancer. She was okay once she understood it was normal. I don't want my daughters and my nieces scared of their bodies, but as they grow up, they do have to know enough to understand the risks." All the children's pediatricians have been informed of their unique family history and the special cancer risk it presents.

"The worst days were when I learned that my sister and my cousin had breast cancer. I was so angry that I had to go through this—I felt victimized by the situation—but I was much more concerned for them than for myself. They were dealing with cancer on a higher level."

The best day came a few months after her sister had finished chemotherapy. "Her hair was growing back, and she said, 'I feel pretty again.' After that we were all able to get on with our lives."

KAREN H.

Karen was in her twenties, married, with a two-year-old daughter, when her mother was diagnosed with breast cancer. "It didn't affect me very much," says Karen. "It was treatable, and it never entered my mind that she would not be okay. She had a mastectomy but no chemotherapy. After a few years, I didn't think about it much." Then her mother's older sister developed cancer and had both breasts removed. Karen knew by then that a family history of breast cancer put her at increased risk, but "I was in my twenties and didn't think it was anything I should be concerned about at the time." A few years later her mother's younger sister had both breasts removed. The fact that this aunt required chemotherapy "scared me," Karen recalls, "but I still wasn't real concerned about myself." Still, Karen and both her sisters began having annual mammograms when they reached 30 because of their family history of breast cancer.

In 1988 Karen started walking for exercise and her mother, who lived nearby, joined her. One morning in September her mother told Karen that she had found a lump in her remaining breast and had made an appointment with the doctor. The lump was malignant, and Karen's mother had a second mastectomy. This time she too required chemotherapy.

In October Karen felt several lumps in her right breast. "I had had an appointment for a mammogram in August, but I canceled it because I was very busy at work. Now it was October, and I was trying to convince myself that I was overreacting to what I felt in my breast. But I did see the doctor. He tried to aspirate one of the lumps, but he got nothing," Karen recalls. The doctor suggested waiting until after Karen's next period to see if the lump changed or disappeared. It did not, and in November he told her she would need a biopsy.

"When I woke up, the first thing I saw was my mother's

face, and I knew immediately that I had breast cancer. I was 33 years old," says Karen. "My mother was more upset about my diagnosis than she had been about either of hers. My emotions were indescribable, but I was more afraid for my life than for the removal of my breast. I just wanted them to get rid of the cancer. I didn't care what they had to do."

Karen's mastectomy was scheduled for the following week. In the meantime, she went to the library and checked out every book she could find about breast cancer. "Reading about it made me feel more in control. I also read [Norman Vincent Peale's] *The Power of Positive Thinking*. From the beginning I was convinced that my attitude was going to be very important."

When she woke up after the mastectomy, "I was bandaged so heavily that I didn't really feel that my breast was gone. It was quite a shock when the bandages finally came off. Still, I was more concerned about the cancer than the removal of my breast. After the operation, the surgeon told me that the lymph nodes looked good, and I took that to mean that they got all the cancer. That weekend my room was filled with flowers and people were pouring in. My spirits were up. I was flying high. But then the surgeon came and stood at the doorway and said, 'Karen, I have some bad news for you. . . . Three of the twelve lymph nodes were positive.' "

It was a crushing blow and meant six months of chemotherapy. "My kids were five and eleven at the time," says Karen. "They had never seen me sick before, and my husband didn't handle it real well. He didn't know how to take over. He was kind of lost. I didn't feel I got a lot of support emotionally from him, and the kids were scared because the two people they were closest to—my mother and myself—were going through chemotherapy at the same time. We had our treatments on Friday and we both were sick all weekend. But we made it through the six months. My mother was done in April of 1989 and I was done in May.

"Every time I would go to the doctor I would want them to tell me I was cancer-free, but they never tell you that. I just had my two-year checkup and asked the doctor about the fact that it has been all this time and no more cancer. . . . He said, 'I wish I could tell you that there would be no more, but I can't.' It is just something that you have to learn to live with."

Breast cancer has changed Karen's life in many ways. During her chemotherapy she decided that she was not happy in her job and decided to return to college. Her reading had convinced her that "I was a very unhappy person. I read a lot about women with breast cancer who were always doing things for other people and never taking care of their own needs. I saw myself in that. So I worked on my self-image and building my self-esteem. I had always been a horrible worrier, and I realized that I had to change. I started praying. I am not a religious person, but I do feel spiritual. So I set aside a time every day, just 15 minutes in the morning, to meditate and pray, not for my life but for guidance and strength to get through one day at a time. It was very beneficial. I was amazed!"

She also separated from her husband. "I felt I was putting everything into my marriage and getting nothing out of it, and I decided not to live like that anymore. I'm a lot happier now."

With meditation and prayer Karen has been making a conscious effort to reduce the stress in her life, and she is trying to instill in her daughter, now a teenager, healthy ways of handling stress. "I think she will have a greater chance to avoid breast cancer if she learns to handle stress better." Karen also has changed her diet. "When I first got married, I had fried foods night after night. I haven't fried a chicken or potatoes in two years now. I try to eat fruits and vegetables and stay away from junk food."

The one thing she has been unable to do for herself is have her remaining breast removed in order to prevent another bout with breast cancer. Her insurance company has refused to pay for the surgery and at present Karen is not in a financial position to assume the cost herself. But, she says, "I still feel that it is an option for me someday."

BUNNY H.

From the time she was a little girl, Bunny realized that there were problems in her family—an awful lot of cancer. Her mother died of a type of digestive tract cancer of unknown origin, her grandmother died of ovarian cancer, and her great-grandmother also died of cancer when she was in her forties. Most of Bunny's great-grandmother's sisters had also died of cancer. In recent years, one by one, Bunny's aunts—her mother's sisters—developed breast or ovarian cancer. Even more cancer—an astonishing amount—came to light when one of Bunny's sisters began to chronicle the family history.

At first the doctors Bunny and her sisters consulted about their own risks dismissed their fears and even suggested that the women might be cancer-phobic. It wasn't until Bunny and her sisters contacted the Creighton Hereditary Cancer Institute that they understood the full extent of their risk: with their family history, all of the women faced a 50 percent risk of breast or ovarian cancer, and the men were considered at high risk of other types of cancer. There already were cases of lung and bladder cancer that had developed at relatively young ages among the men, an indication of a hereditary component to the diseases.

Any lingering doubts about the risk to Bunny's generation disappeared when, within a year of each other, two of her sisters, both in their early thirties, developed breast cancer.

"I have four boys, and when I realized the risk the women

in this family face, I thought, 'Thank God, my sons aren't going to be affected.' But they are!" In addition to the heightened cancer risk for women in the family, the strength of the hereditary cancer pattern in the family suggested that the men were capable of carrying the gene responsible for all the breast and ovarian cancer and passing it to their daughters.

Bunny has told her sons that they have to be aware that "this is a problem for all of us. I have emphasized to my 21-year-old that when he gets serious about a young woman and is contemplating marriage, he has to be honest with her about his odds of being a gene carrier." Her son's daughters might be at very high risk for breast and ovarian cancer. Still, she hopes that researchers soon will find the gene responsible for hereditary cancer. "Then they might be able to find a way to stop the gene from expressing itself," says Bunny. "Hopefully, my kids will not have to go through this."

When she understood the extent of her own risk, Bunny followed medical advice and decided to have her breasts and ovaries removed. But she had taken precautions long before then. "I told my husband that because there was so much cancer in my family, I didn't want to have any more children after I passed 30. I wanted to be sure I was around to raise my kids. My husband understood. His mother died of breast cancer when he was 14, so he had no problem with my decision."

"You do begin to face life that way," says Bunny philosophically. "I don't know what is going to happen, but I want to see my kids through high school. Anything beyond that is a bonus." Recently, her 17-year-old son remarked that most of his friends had not yet experienced a single death in their families, but that "we no more than recover from one death than we have another death or diagnosis to deal with."

"I can feel his pain," says Bunny, "but I try to get my kids to look at the positive aspects, at how close a family we are, at how we are able to talk to each other about things other families can never discuss, how we have learned to be supportive, and to appreciate life and how precious it is."

CHAPTER

8

Personality, Attitude, and Cancer

AN increasingly popular view of cancer holds that stress, emotional health, and even personality can predispose a person to the disease or determine who recovers and who does not. This notion stems in part from very exciting new research that is just beginning to reveal links between the brain and central nervous system and the immune system, which protects our bodies from disease. Some of this research has led to fascinating findings that would seem to confirm that stress, emotional factors, and, perhaps, personality do make a difference in who gets sick and who gets well. So far none of this new data demonstrate a conclusive link between disease, attitude, emotional health, and personality, although much of it makes compelling food for thought about the strength of mind-body connections.

HOW THE MIND AFFECTS THE BODY

There is little doubt that what goes on in our minds can affect us physically. Fear makes us tremble, embarrassment makes us blush, tension makes us clench our teeth or our fists. It also gives us headaches, backaches, and upset stomachs. Cancer patients who have become nauseated in response to chemotherapy have gotten sick in the stomach at the mere sight of the nurse or technician who administers the drug.

Doctors have long recognized the power of the mind over the body. How else can we explain the placebo effect—the uncontested medical fact that a hefty percentage of any group of people given a harmless pill will recover from whatever ails them? There even have been some cancer remissions that only the placebo effect can explain. Perhaps the most famous was reported in 1957 in the Journal of Prospective Techniques by Bruno Klopfer, M.D. He told about a terminally ill patient, let's call him Mr. X, who read about the drug Krebiozen which was then being touted as a new cure for cancer and begged his doctor to try it. The physician had his doubts but decided a single injection couldn't hurt such a sick man. To the doctor's amazement, within days Mr. X was up, dressed, and strolling around the hospital. Tests showed that his tumors had miraculously shrunk! Months later Krebiozen made the news again—the drug had turned out to be ineffective. Mr. X, again on the brink of death, checked into the hospital. This time his doctor offered him a new, improved form of Krebiozen but actually administered a harmless solution. Again the cancer symptoms vanished, and Mr. X went home an apparently healthy man. Eventually the final medical verdict on Krebiozen hit the headlines: it was completely worthless. Mr. X's cancer returned, and he died.

We all have some appreciation of the toll stress can take on health. It has been linked to disorders ranging from backaches to ulcers, heart attacks, and cancer. The new science of psychoneuroimmunology (PNI) focuses on unearthing the links between stress, emotions, personality, and physical disease. The word itself tells you a little bit about the approach to these studies—*psycho* refers to the mind, *neuro* refers to the nervous system, and *immunology* refers to the immune system. Researchers in this field have turned up some intriguing data about the effect of stress and emotional states on the immune system. They have measured varying levels of certain immune system substances in the blood and saliva and compared them with levels of stress and various emotional states. One study by Steven Schleifer, MD, of Mount Sinai School of Medicine in New York found that the immune responses of men whose wives died or were dying of breast cancer declined in the months preceding and following their wives' deaths. Another, by David McClelland, Ph.D. of Harvard University found that levels of immunoglobulin A, an immune system substance in saliva that serves as our first line of defense against cold viruses, rose temporarily in college students immediately after they watched a film about Mother Theresa's altruistic work in Calcutta.

DEPRESSION AND CANCER

A number of studies have suggested that depressed, emotionally repressed, or passive individuals are more likely to develop cancer than those in more robust mental health and with higher self-esteem. A lot of this work is very persuasive. One of the most telling studies was done with medical students at Johns Hopkins University in Baltimore. For 30 years researcher Caroline Thomas collected physical and psychological data on the students and asked them to respond every year to questions about their health. When she evaluated all of the data, Dr. Thomas found that the students who developed cancer later in life were emotionally detached from their parents, had more negative attitudes about their families, and tended to bottle up their emotions. These characteristics showed up as depression.

Other studies have found that people who manifest a sense of hopelessness and lack of control over their lives are more likely to develop cancer than those whose attitudes are more positive and upbeat.

While intriguing, these findings have been challenged by critics who offer persuasive arguments. Skeptics note that, in the first place, relating depression to cancer after the disease develops holds certain perils. Wouldn't it be normal for people with cancer to be depressed? Most of us would agree that cancer is a pretty good reason for feeling down in the dumps, and blaming depression for cancer may be putting the cart before the horse. Second, depression is a symptom of some forms of cancer. Patients with pancreatic cancer, for instance, are often depressed. And there is little doubt that cancer's physical effect on the nervous system and hormonal balance may lead to depression. So, does depression predispose to cancer or does cancer predispose to depression? Or is there any connection at all?

The latest word on the subject comes from a study by researchers at the National Institute on Aging in which more than 6,400 people participated. All were evaluated for symptoms of depression and then followed for 10 years. The researchers found that 11 percent of the depressed participants and 10 percent of those with no symptoms of depression eventually developed cancer.

The authors of the study concluded that their results "call into question the causal connection between depressive symptoms" and cancer. One expert in the field, Bernard H. Fox, Ph.D., of the Boston University School of Medicine, agrees. In a 1989 editorial in the *Journal of the American Medical Association* (August 31, 1989) he maintained that most of the earlier studies linking cancer with depression "suffered from faulty design, small samples . . . and a number of biases." Although Fox doesn't regard any of the evidence gathered so far as conclusive, he noted that most studies suggest "that any causal link between depressive symptoms and cancer risk is either weak or does not exist at all."

CANCER AND PERSONALITY

The idea that there may be a cancer-prone personality stems from studies by Lydia Temoshok, a psychologist at the University of California School of Medicine in San Francisco. In interviewing patients with malignant melanoma, a potentially fatal type of skin cancer, she found that most shared certain personality traits: they were nice people, model patients who were rather passive and never expressed negative emotions. She described them as Type C personalities (as distinct from Type A personalities, thought by some experts to be at higher risk for heart disease, and Type B personalities, who are rated at lower risk for heart disease). Over time Temoshok found the Type C patients were less likely to respond well to treatment than patients who were able to express strong emotions and feel anger, fear, or sadness.

Since then a number of theories about the personalities and attitudes of cancer patients have surfaced. Although most researchers do not believe that your personality can predispose you to cancer, there remains some evidence that survivors tend to be fighters. In their study of women with breast cancer psychiatrist H. Steven Geer, M.D. and Tina Morris of King's College Hospital in London found that the ones who recover tend to be those who resolve to "beat this thing" and those who react to news of their cancer by denying that anything is wrong. Women who do less well respond in one of two ways: with a stoic, stiff-upper-lip attitude, they go about their lives as if nothing has changed, or they give in to hopelessness. Observations that attitude makes a difference to the survival of cancer patients were tested in a 1985 study by psychologist Barrie Cassileth and a team of researchers at the University of Pennsylvania. Their results showed no correlation between mental state and progression of the cancer. But critics of Cassileth's study argue that its results might have been different if she and her team had focused on patients whose disease had not already spread.

The case is far from closed on the question of how state of mind influences recovery from cancer. Nevertheless, some doctors firmly believe—although they recognize that there is no good scientific data to back them up—that certain personality types are more prone to cancer.

BLAMING THE VICTIM

The idea that a negative attitude or depression plays a role in developing cancer or other diseases has a disturbing flip side. It has led to all sorts of approaches to dealing with cancer that may or may not help, including meditation, laughter, and visualizing cancer cells being zapped by the immune system's warrior white blood cells. There is a wealth of anecdotal evidence that some or all of these techniques work. Since we do know that feeling in control does seem to help people cope with illness, anything that provides a sense of control can only be viewed as useful. But what happens when a patient tries some of these techniques and cancer recurs? Does that mean that the patient has failed? Or hasn't tried hard enough? Or chose the wrong method? Or lacks the will to live?

In a 1985 editorial in the *New England Journal of Medicine,* editor Marcia Angell, M.D., raised these questions and observed that the "medical profession also participates in the tendency to hold the patient responsible for his [sic] progress. In our desire to pay tribute to gallantry and grace in the face of hardship, we sometimes credit these qualities with cures, not realizing that we may also be implying blame when there are reverses."

Dr. Angell took a very hard line on the question of how profoundly the mind influences the body: "It is time to acknowledge that our belief in disease as a direct reflection of mental state is largely folklore. Furthermore, the corollary view of sickness and death as a personal failure is a particularly unfortunate form of blaming the victim. At a time when patients are already burdened by disease, they should not be further burdened by having to accept responsibility for the outcome."

Many physicians and researchers would dispute Dr. Angell's assertion that the belief in disease being a reflection of mental state is "largely folklore." But it is hard to argue with the point she makes about blaming the victim. We don't know what causes cancer. We know what some of the various risk factors are. We know what malignant cells look like, and we can predict, with some degree of accuracy, the course of different stages of the disease. New findings about mind-body connections add another dimension to our knowledge, but there are still many more questions about cancer than answers. It would be tragic and very wrong for any woman to blame her personality, attitude, or emotional state for her breast or ovarian cancer. And although it may be helpful to encourage a patient to feel in control of her body and her cancer, it would also be cruel and inhumane for anyone to suggest to her that she is responsible in any way for getting sick or for not getting better.

CHAPTER

9

Treatment Options

I F you do develop cancer, you face some big decisions about what to do next. Women with breast cancer have more options for treatment than women with ovarian cancer, but that does not mean the choices are easy.

BREAST CANCER

A biopsy may be all the breast surgery you need. But if the entire lump isn't removed during the biopsy, you will need more surgery and after that, perhaps, follow-up treatment (radiation therapy, chemotherapy, or hormone therapy) to destroy any breast cancer cells that may remain in the body. Breast cancer can't kill you if it is confined to the breast; the danger is that by the time a lump is found and diagnosed as malignant, some cells may have traveled beyond the breast to establish beachheads elsewhere in the body. When breast cancer spreads, it usually attacks the bones, liver, lungs, and brain. Because of this threat, you want to know as much as you can about your cancer as soon as it is diagnosed. A variety of laboratory tests should be done to assess how aggressive the cancer is and how likely it is to have spread beyond the breast. The results can help you and your doctor decide upon the most appropriate treatment. Some of these tests may have been performed during the biopsy that determined that the lump was malignant.

WHAT THE BIOPSY SHOWS

A biopsy can tell you much more than whether a lump is benign or malignant. If cancer is present, tests run as part of the biopsy can show whether the lump originated in the ducts or the lobes of the breasts. (Eighty-six percent of all breast cancer begins in the ducts.) The biopsy report also will state whether the cancer is invasive or is an in situ precancer. (See Chapter 3 for a discussion of carcinoma in situ and its treatment. In this chapter, we will focus on invasive cancer.)

The pathologist who does the biopsy can determine what type of breast cancer you have. As you learned in Chapter 3, there are several kinds. Of these, mucinous, papillary, or tubular tumors are the least aggressive and the least likely to have spread. However, less than 10 percent of all breast tumors fall into one of these three categories.

The biopsy also will reveal something about the characteristics of the cancer cells. Better developed or "differentiated" cancer cells that don't look very different from normal cells tend to be less aggressive than poorly differentiated cells, which, under the microscope, look disorganized and wild.

The biopsy can also yield the following information:

- Whether or not cancer cells have entered any blood or lymphatic vessels, expressed on the report as vascular (blood vessel) or lymphatic invasion. The outlook is better if the pathologist finds no signs of these invasions.
- Whether or not any dead cancer cells are present. Usually regarded as a bad sign, dead cancer cells indicate that the tumor has outgrown its blood supply.

But the most important biopsy finding has to do with the tumor's hormonal status—whether or not it depends on estrogen for growth.

Estrogen Receptor Assay

The estrogen receptor assay should always be performed during the biopsy. This essential test tells you whether the cancer cells have receptors for estrogen. Receptors are structures on the surface of cells, usually described as biochemical locks that only a specific body chemical key can open. No hormone or other chemical can enter any human cell without attaching to the specific receptor designed for it. In this respect, the receptors are indeed like locks. When the correct chemical "key" meets the receptor, the two bind together, giving the chemical access to the cell.

During the estrogen receptor assay, the pathologist looks for receptors for both estrogen and progesterone. The presence of both indicates that the estrogen receptors are functioning properly and that the tumor is indeed estrogen-dependent. The biopsy report will state whether a tumor is estrogen receptor (ER) negative or positive. Most breast cancers are ER positive. In general, postmenopausal women are more likely to have ER positive tumors than are premenopausal women. In addition to stating whether a tumor is ER positive or negative, the biopsy report usually will state whether the tumor is ER "rich" or "poor."

The long-term outlook usually is better when a breast cancer tumor is ER positive. These tumors tend to be less aggressive than ER negative cancers.

You should make sure that an estrogen receptor assay is done at the time of biopsy. These days it usually is, but to be certain, ask your surgeon in advance about the tests to be performed during the biopsy if the lump turns out to be malignant. Insist upon an estrogen receptor assay. The lump removed at biopsy is the only source of information about whether the cancer is estrogen-dependent. Once it is out, no easily identifiable cancer cells remain to test for hormonal status. This information is vital to determining the course of treatment—whether chemotherapy or hormone therapy is most appropriate. Estrogen receptor assays must be done *immediately* after the lump is removed. Tissue from the lump must be frozen for the test. For this reason, the biopsy itself should be done in a hospital where a pathologist is available.

New Tests

Several new tests just beginning to come into wide use yield more valuable information about long-term outlook.

Nuclear Grade Test: This test assesses how actively cancer cells are dividing. The speed and quantity of dividing cells determines how aggressive the cancer is. Although it can tell doctors a lot about what they are up against in treating the cancer, the nuclear grade evaluation is not routinely done. It takes a pathologist experienced in establishing nuclear grade to get worthwhile results.

DNA Flow Cytometry: This test measures the tumor's DNA content. When the amount is normal, the tumor cells are described as diploid. More aggressive cancers tend to have aneuploid cells, meaning that they have too much or too little DNA. Flow cytometry can also determine the percentage of cancer cells that are dividing at any one time. This is expressed as a high or low *s phase fraction.* The higher the *s phase fraction,* the more aggressive the tumor. There are still questions about the importance of knowing whether tumor cells are aneuploid or diploid, but the *s phase fraction* helps in assessing the general outlook.

Cathepsin D Test: This very promising new test measures the amount of cathepsin D, a protein secreted by tumor cells. New studies have shown that the more cathepsin D secreted, the greater the likelihood that cancer will recur. However, more research is needed to determine how accurate a barometer cathepsin D is for cancer recurrence.

STAGES OF BREAST CANCER

The more doctors know about the extent of the cancer, the more accurately they can target treatment. Most women know that early breast cancer detection enhances the long-term outlook. For instance, very small tumors (one centimeter or less—see Figure 9.1 to get an idea of size) have a very good outlook—the recurrence rate is less than 10 percent in 10 years. Luckily, today most breast cancer is found relatively early in its course.

Considering that breast cancer usually has been around for six to eight years before it can be detected, you might be skeptical about what constitutes "early." Over the years experts have devised criteria, based on three factors, for the various stages of breast cancer:

- The size of the tumor
- Whether or not the cancer cells have traveled to the lymph nodes, and if so, how many lymph nodes are positive for cancer
- Whether or not the cancer has metastasized—spread beyond the breast

After evaluating these three factors, a doctor can classify breast cancer as stage I, II, III, or IV. Let's take a look at what these four stages mean.

Stage I

A Stage I tumor is small (less than two centimeters in diameter), has not involved the lymph nodes, and has not detectably spread beyond the breast.

The best indication of whether or not cancer has metastasized comes from evaluation of the lymph nodes in the armpit. These nodes can become noticeably enlarged—you can feel them—when cancer cells reach them. But some enlarged nodes show no signs of cancer when they are removed and examined. And nodes that don't feel enlarged to

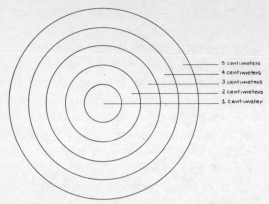

Figure 9.1. Tumor Sizes (*Source: National Cancer Institute*)

the surgeon's touch may still harbor cancer cells. For this reason, surgeons typically remove at least 15 lymph nodes during surgery for breast cancer. If all are clear, or "node-negative," you can assume that the remaining nodes are also cancer-free. But you cannot be absolutely sure that the cancer has not spread: about 25 percent of all women whose nodes are negative go on to develop more cancer again later. Still, most node-negative cancers never recur.

Metastasis can be determined by a variety of diagnostic procedures and scans to test for the presence of other signs of cancer elsewhere in the body. Because spreading breast cancer typically moves to the lungs, liver, bones, and brain, these organs are the ones doctors focus on first. Sometimes symptoms such as bone pain, headaches, or loss of appetite suggest a problem elsewhere in the body. Blood tests can show whether or not you are anemic, a possible indication of metastasis. Liver function studies done from blood samples can help determine whether the liver is affected.

A chest X-ray can reveal lung cancer. In a bone scan the patient is injected with radioactive particles and, a few hours later, lies under a machine that produces images of the skeleton by "reading" the radioactive particles. These particles will show up better in areas where bone is changing, indicating that something is going on. Unfortunately, a bone scan doesn't show what the trouble is—whether it is arthritis, cancer, or an infection.

If anything suspicious shows up on any of these exams, more sophisticated tests will be administered, including:

- a liver scan (similar to the bone scan) if liver function is abnormal
- a CAT (computerized axial tomography) scan, which gives very detailed cross-sectional pictures of the organ being examined
- an MRI (magnetic resonance imaging) of the brain which produces three-dimensional images.

If all the tests and scans are negative, you can assume—although you can't be certain—that the cancer hasn't spread to distant sites in your body. You can't be positive because, sophisticated as some of the tests are, they cannot pick up microscopic cancers. They can only reveal signs of more advanced disease.

Stage II

Although still considered early, Stage II cancers are slightly more serious than Stage I cancers, and the criteria are a bit more ambiguous:

- a small (between one and two centimeters) tumor with some positive lymph nodes; or
- a tumor from two to five centimeters with positive *or* negative nodes; or
- a tumor larger than five centimeters with negative nodes; and
- with any of these kinds of tumors, no metastasis.

Stage III

Stage III includes large tumors with positive lymph nodes and large tumors with any one of the following "grave signs"—indications that cancer cells probably have spread beyond the breast although tests have not positively revealed metastasis:

- Swelling of the skin (edema) over the tumor
- "Peau d'orange" (orange peel)—a puffiness that makes the skin of the breast resemble an orange peel
- A tumor that is ulcerating through the skin
- A tumor that is stuck to the chest wall and does not move
- Walnut-sized lymph nodes in the armpit
- Swollen lymph nodes above the collarbone
- Red and infected-looking skin around the lump

Stage IV

Stage IV includes all breast cancers that have spread, regardless of tumor size and the presence of positive or negative lymph nodes.

The stage of cancer diagnosis is the most important consideration when deciding on treatment. You will be happy to learn that today the vast majority of breast cancer is at Stage I or II at the time of diagnosis. These cases are highly treatable. The five-year survival rate is 80 percent for women with Stage I breast cancer, and about 65 percent for women with Stage II breast cancer. The outlook is less promising for Stage III breast cancer, although about 40 percent of all women diagnosed at this stage survive for five years. As you might imagine, women whose cancer has spread far beyond the breast at the time of detection face bleaker prospects. But luckily, only a small percentage of women fall into this category.

SURGERY

If you are diagnosed with breast cancer, you are going to need at least two and perhaps three surgical procedures:

- The biopsy to establish diagnosis (If you have had an excisional biopsy [see Chapter 5] and opt for lumpectomy, you may not need further surgery on your breast.)
- An operation to remove lymph nodes from the underarm (axilla) to help determine the stage of your disease
- Another operation to remove more of the lump or more surrounding tissue (margins), or if appropriate, a mastectomy

As you undoubtedly know, surgery for breast cancer has changed enormously during the past decade. The dreaded and disfiguring Halstead radical mastectomy, which removed the breast, all of the underarm lymph nodes, some fat and skin, and muscles overlying the chest, is rarely done these days. Initially, it was replaced by the modified radical mastectomy, which removes the breast, the lymph nodes under the arm, and the lining over the chest muscles (leaving the muscles intact). The modified radical mastectomy is the most common operation for breast cancer today. However, lumpectomy—removal of the lump—is beginning to gain ground, and rightly so. Not only does it preserve the breast but, more important, women who have lumpectomies survive just as long as women who have mastectomies. Indeed, in a 1990 consensus statement on the treatment of early breast cancer, a group of experts convened by the National Institutes of Health (NIH) rated lumpectomy as the "preferable" surgery because "it provides survival equivalent to total mastectomy and also preserves the breast."

Of course, there are certain medical exceptions to any general rule. Lumpectomy is not always appropriate, even for some women with Stage I or II breast cancer. It is not the best treatment, for example, for women who have large lumps in small breasts. By the time the tumor and surrounding healthy margins are removed there may not be enough breast left for a normal appearance. Lumpectomy is also inappropriate when more than one malignant lump exists or when cancer picked up on a mammogram occurs as microcalcifications—tiny spots of cancer scattered or diffused through the breast. The cancer may indeed be early and survival prospects excellent, but the physical layout of the cancer in the breast precludes a lumpectomy.

Ironically, lumpectomy may be the surgery of choice for women with Stage IV cancer that already has spread to other body parts. In these cases, surgery takes a backseat to other forms of treatment—chemotherapy and radiation—to control the cancer. Since the cancer already has spread, it becomes less important to get the original lump out of the breast. A mastectomy simply wouldn't help matters—the damage has been done. But a lumpectomy to get rid of the original tumor may be recommended. Cancer this advanced is rarely cured, but sometimes it can be controlled for a while—possibly indefinitely—with chemotherapy.

These days mastectomy usually is recommended for women with Stage III breast cancer because their lumps are large and some "grave signs" may be present.

Removing the Lymph Nodes

Once a lump has been removed for biopsy, no further surgery on the breast may be needed, although if laboratory studies find cancer in the margins of tissue surrounding the lump, the surgeon may recommend taking out a slightly wider margin. This will in any case mean more surgery a few days after the initial operation (it usually takes a few days to complete all of the lab studies involved in a biopsy). Another operation will be needed to remove lymph nodes from the underarm to determine whether the cancer has started to spread. This surgery requires an incision across the armpit, is done under a general anesthetic, and requires spending one to three days in the hospital.

Removal of lymph nodes is not without its complications. Most women develop some swelling afterward, and a nerve may be severed or stretched, resulting in some permanent numbness in the back of the armpit. This won't limit the use of the arm, but it does affect sensation. Less common complications include pain in the arm due to an inflammation of a vein, swelling of the arm (as opposed to swelling of the armpit), and even more rarely, nerve injury that affects the way the arm works.

Only You Can Decide

Choosing the type of surgery is not entirely a medical decision. It is a very personal one that each woman must make for herself. How you feel about yourself, your body, and cancer will influence your choice. Some women are more afraid of losing a breast than of cancer and would not consider a mastectomy unless convinced it was the only way to save their lives. Others are so terrified by cancer that they cannot bear the thought that a single cell might linger in the affected breast; they would rather lose the breast than live with the uncertainty. It is not a decision to be made lightly or hastily. A woman who has a lumpectomy and regrets her decision can always have her breast removed. But a mastectomy is permanent—although breast reconstruction can be done, it will not, however good, bring back the breast you lost. Obviously, the more information you have about your cancer and your prospects, the better prepared you will be to make the choice that's right for you.

Some surgeons have strong opinions about which operation is best and may try to influence you one way or the other. Bear in mind that doctors are not always entirely objective. An old-fashioned surgeon with strong opinions as to what kind of operation is best for you may be very reassuring. But this kind of surgeon may be biased in favor of the operation he or she is most accustomed to performing. Similarly, a doctor who believes strongly in breast preservation may not fully appreciate the reasons why you may be more comfortable with mastectomy. Whatever the doctor's bias, if you are a candidate for lumpectomy (that is, your case is *not* one of the exceptions mentioned above), you must understand that the surgery will be *just as good as mastectomy* in helping you recover from cancer.

However, some women still choose mastectomy because most patients who have lumpectomies must also have radiation therapy, a six-week course of treatment aimed at zapping any cancer cells left in the breast. We'll discuss radiation in more detail later in this chapter.

Why should the need for radiation therapy influence a woman's decision? First of all, the six-week course of treatment requires going to the hospital five days a week for six weeks. If you live far from the hospital, the daily grind may be too inconvenient and too disruptive. Some women would rather have the mastectomy, go home, recover, and get on with their lives. When Nancy Reagan developed breast cancer while living in the White House, she chose mastectomy over lumpectomy for exactly this reason. She did not feel she could take time out from her duties as First Lady to stay at home in Washington for six weeks in order to go in to the hospital for the daily radiation treatments. Mrs. Reagan has spoken very candidly about her choice, and she certainly can't be faulted for making it. It was the right one for her at that point in her life. But had she chosen lumpectomy, her decision would have gone a long way toward allaying lingering public doubts about lumpectomy being as good a treatment for early breast cancer as mastectomy.

Before making any decision about surgery, it is a good idea to get a second medical opinion. Some insurance plans *require* you to do this, and it always helps to get additional input. Don't worry about hurting your surgeon's feelings— you won't be the first patient to seek a second opinion. In fact, a good doctor should encourage you to talk to another doctor before making up your mind. There is no great rush—taking a week or two to get more information and a second opinion won't hurt. Remember, however, that no doctor can decide for you. All a physician can do is present the alternatives, disclose any personal bias toward one type of surgery over another, and answer any questions you have about the surgery itself and other treatment you may or may not need.

RADIATION

Research has shown that less than 10 percent of women who have lumpectomies and the six-week course of radiation therapy develop a second cancer in the same breast, compared with about 39 percent of those who have a lumpectomy but no radiation. Radiation affects only the breast—it doesn't do anything to protect against cancer developing elsewhere in the body as a result of cells migrating beyond the breast.

The idea of radiation may worry you—after all, as we explained in Chapter 1, some women develop breast cancer as a result of exposure to radiation. It does seem a bit contradictory that something that can cause cancer can also cure or control it. But with radiation administered for therapeutic purposes—to destroy any wayward cancer cells remaining in the breast—the amounts are very carefully calculated and targeted to minimize the chance that radiation will trigger more cancer. The risk isn't zero, but the benefits of radiation therapy by far outweigh the remote chance that the treatment will cause cancer.

After the six weeks of daily radiation treatments, you may be given a "boost" of extra radiation aimed at the site of the lump. This may be done with a radioactive implant temporarily placed in your breast or by a type of external radiation slightly different from what was used during the six-week course. The implant is a series of very thin plastic tubes containing iridium seeds, tiny radioactive pellets. While the implant is in, you are radioactive—that is, your body gives off radiation that can be picked up by others. You certainly would not want to be around a pregnant woman or young children, so as a rule you have to check into the hospital while the implant is in place, usually about 36 hours. You can have visitors, but many hospitals do not permit pregnant women or children under the age of 18 to visit patients with radiation implants. Other visitors are okay, but they should sit at least five feet away from the bed and stay for only a short time. Nurses and others on the hospital staff who care for you will try to answer your questions from the doorway and take care of your physical needs quickly to minimize their exposure. After all, they deal with many patients with implants and must take precautions to reduce their own exposure.

When the boost is administered externally instead of via an implant, you do not have to go to the hospital. You just go back to the radiation therapist for a few extra days. The boost is administered via an electron beam, a type of radioactive particle that does not penetrate deeply. The radiation dose is not as high as the one that can be delivered via an implant. External boosts generally are recommended when the tumor was not very deep.

Side Effects

Radiation does cause a number of side effects. The ones lumpectomy patients are most likely to experience are reddening of the skin similar to a sunburn, itching under the breast or armpit, and soreness and swelling from fluid buildup in the breast. These side effects will disappear on their own, usually before treatment is over. Many women complain of moderate to intense fatigue. Some are wiped out; others can get through the day easily enough but feel very tired in the evening. Fatigue may not end when treatment does, but in time it will disappear.

Radiation aimed at the breast does not cause hair loss (although radiation can lead to hair loss if it is used to treat cancer of the head or neck).

SYSTEMIC TREATMENTS

Systemic treatment is therapy designed to eliminate any cancer cells that have traveled beyond the breast. It includes the dreaded chemotherapy (the use of powerful anticancer drugs), and hormone therapy, a very effective type of treatment when the cancer is ER positive. Both treatments are also used to combat advanced cancer and metastatic breast cancer, but that is beyond the scope of this book. Here we are concerned with "adjuvant" systemic therapy—chemotherapy or hormone therapy used as a follow-up to either lumpectomy plus radiation or mastectomy to eliminate any cancer cells that may have traveled beyond the breast.

Chemotherapy

The drugs used against cancer are cytotoxic, which literally means that they kill cells. The most effective course of chemotherapy probably doesn't kill all cancer cells, but it cuts down their numbers to a level at which the immune system can destroy the remaining ones on its own.

The trouble with chemotherapy is that it kills all cells that divide rapidly. These include hair and bone marrow cells as well as cancer cells. Although you may be most concerned about knocking off the hair cells and the hair loss that follows, the effect on the bone marrow cells can be dangerous. Without sufficient bone marrow cells, your body cannot produce blood cells. Because of the threat to the bone marrow, chemotherapy has to be spaced out over months so that between treatments the bone marrow has a chance to recover from the onslaught of the drugs. Of course, this rest and recuperation also gives cancer cells a chance to recoup. So the aim of chemotherapy is to kill off as many cancer cells as possible without killing the patient. This sounds pretty crude, and it is. Someday we may have drugs that kill only cancer cells without harming healthy cells in the body. But until that time comes we'll have to do the best we can with the drugs available. Side effects to the contrary, the cytotoxic drugs now in use can save your life.

Who Gets Chemotherapy?

Adjuvant chemotherapy can be life-saving, but it isn't always necessary. The great dilemma today is deciding who needs it and who can do without it.

Until recently, adjuvant chemotherapy was recommended only for women who have positive lymph nodes, on the theory that cancer cells have traveled beyond the breast and have to be eliminated if possible. This makes sense, and today most women with positive lymph nodes do get some form of systemic treatment. But chemotherapy doesn't seem to work very well in postmenopausal women with ER positive tumors. They do much better with hormone therapy, which we'll discuss below. The current dilemma is whether to offer adjuvant chemotherapy to women with negative nodes. For 70 percent of them, mastectomy or lumpectomy with radiation will do the trick—their cancer will never recur. But we do know that cancer eventually will recur in about 30 percent of node-negative women. The trouble is, we have no way of telling whom it will be. You can see the problem: Do we subject all these women to the ravages of chemotherapy when only 30 percent need it? Or do we just present the odds and let patients decide for themselves? We know that chemotherapy will cut the odds of recurrence by 30 percent—that is, 20 percent, not 30 percent, of node-negative women will experience a recurrence. Clearly, a major challenge to researchers is finding some reliable means of distinguishing node-negative women whose cancer will recur from the majority who are cured with mastectomy or lumpectomy with radiation.

The NIH consensus statement offered some guidelines on the worrisome subject of who should and who should not get adjuvant systemic therapy. It advised doctors to tell patients about the benefits and risks and to make sure their patients understand the odds of recurrence and the side effects of chemotherapy. The consensus statement also noted that node-negative patients with tumors one centimeter or less in size are at very low risk for recurrence (less than 10 percent over 10 years) and do not require adjuvant therapy.

Hormone Therapy

Postmenopausal breast cancer patients with ER positive tumors usually are treated with adjuvant hormone therapy (instead of chemotherapy)—with the drug tamoxifen, which interferes with the locking function of the estrogen receptors on the cancer cells. Tamoxifen jams the receptors, preventing estrogen from entering the cancer cell and fostering its growth. Deprived of this biochemical nutrient, the cell dies. The good news about tamoxifen is that it does not have the uncomfortable side effects of cytotoxic drugs. Studies have also shown that it leads to a 50 percent decrease in deaths from coronary heart disease. The bad news is that it may have long-term effects that we haven't encountered since tamoxifen was introduced in 1973. Animal studies have found an association between large doses of tamoxifen and the development of liver and ovarian cancers, but studies in humans have not found an increased risk of these diseases at the doses usually recommended for treatment of women with breast cancer. (What happens in animals does not always happen in humans.) The NIH consensus statement had this to say about the use of tamoxifen by postmenopausal women with ER positive cancer: "The overall benefits . . . clearly outweigh any toxicities currently described." At this point the most worrisome potential long-term side effects of tamoxifen seem restricted to premenopausal women with ER positive breast cancer.

Studies now in progress suggest that a combination of tamoxifen and chemotherapy may be more effective than tamoxifen alone.

Tamoxifen is taken orally in pill form twice a day. Treatment continues for two to five years. Although most women have no side effects, some experience hot flashes, transient nausea, and vaginal spotting. Less common side effects include vaginal itching, bleeding, or discharge, depression, loss of appetite, and headaches. Premenopausal women will stop menstruating and may develop ovarian cysts. Even though they do not menstruate, they do ovulate and will need protection against pregnancy. (The effects of tamoxifen on a developing fetus are not known.)

Still, the anticancer effects of tamoxifen are so striking that in 1991 the National Cancer Institute announced a five-year study involving 16,000 women to see if the drug can prevent breast cancer. (To qualify for the study, you must be 60 years old or have a risk equivalent to that of a 60-year-old woman with normal risk factors. For example, a 40-year-old woman whose mother had breast cancer has a risk equivalent to that of a 60-year-old.) Half the women will take tamoxifen, and half will take a dummy pill. If results show that women in the tamoxifen group have a significantly lower rate of cancer than the women on the dummy pill, all women may be advised to take tamoxifen for the rest of their lives.

OVARIAN CANCER

As we discussed in Chapter 5, diagnosing ovarian cancer frequently requires exploratory surgery. The surgeon usually removes the diseased ovaries as well as the uterus, the fallopian tubes, and any abnormal fluid or tissue in the abdomen. The surgery also provides vital information for staging the disease. Findings from other diagnostic tests prior to surgery also help to establish the stage the cancer has reached. In Chapter 5 we reviewed the tests available to detect ovarian cancer. Here we will take a look at some additional procedures that may be ordered when there is a strong suspicion that the disease is present.

DIAGNOSTIC PROCEDURES

In addition to the pelvic examination and an ultrasound exam (described in Chapter 5), a woman with symptoms of ovarian cancer will need a number of tests to determine whether the disease has spread to the abdomen, lungs, liver, bladder, kidneys, urinary tract, or bowel:

- A chest X-ray
- A CAT scan of the abdomen, liver, and lungs
- An IVP (intravenous pyleogram), an X-ray study of the kidneys, ureters, and bladder (A contrast dye is injected into the bloodstream before the X-ray to illuminate any abnormalities in the kidneys, ureters, and bladder.)
- A barium enema (lower GI series) to evaluate the urinary tract and large bowel (The patient swallows barium, a chalky substance that provides contrast on the X-rays to reveal abnormal growths and narrowed or displaced areas in the large intestine.)

The results of these tests and the extent of the cancer revealed by surgery are combined to arrive at a determination of the stage of the disease.

STAGES OF OVARIAN CANCER

A number of years ago a committee of the International Federation of Gynecology and Obstetrics developed a system for staging ovarian cancer. Treatment depends on which stage best describes the cancer:

Stage I: Cancer is limited to the ovaries.

Stage IA: Cancer is limited to one ovary; there is no ascites (fluid accumulation in the abdomen) and no tumor on the external surface of the ovary; the capsule surrounding the ovary is intact.

Stage IB: Cancer is found in both ovaries; there is no fluid in the abdomen and no cancer on the outer surfaces of the ovaries; the ovarian capsules are intact.

Stage IC: The tumor is on one or both ovaries and *one* of the following characteristics is present: cancer is on the outer surface of one or both ovaries; the ovarian capsule is ruptured; abdominal fluid is present or the fluid used to wash the abdomen during surgery contains cancer cells.

Stage II: Cancer is in one or both ovaries and has spread to the uterus, fallopian tubes, or other tissues in the pelvis.

Stage IIA: Cancer has spread to the uterus and/or the fallopian tubes.

Stage IIB: Cancer has spread to other pelvic tissues.

Stage IIC: Cancer has spread to the pelvis and *one* of the following characteristics is present: cancer is on the outer surface of one or both ovaries; the capsule has ruptured; abdominal fluid is present or cancer cells are found in abdominal washings. (The abdominal "wash" is discussed at the end of the next section.)

Stage III: Cancer is present in both ovaries and has spread to the lymph nodes in the abdomen or to the outer surface of the liver, intestine, or other abdominal organs.

Stage IIIA: Cancer is limited to the pelvis; the lymph nodes are not involved, but there are microscopic deposits of cancer cells on the outer surfaces of abdominal organs.

Stage IIIB: Cancer is limited to the pelvis; the lymph nodes are negative, but there is cancer not larger than two centimeters on abdominal organs.

Stage IIIC: The cancer affecting the abdomen is larger than two centimeters and/or lymph nodes positive for cancer have been found.

Stage IV: One or both ovaries are affected, and the cancer has spread to the inside of the liver or other abdominal organs or to organs outside the abdomen.

SURGERY

Surgery for ovarian cancer usually involves hysterectomy (removal of the uterus) and bilateral salpingo-oophorectomy (removal of the ovaries and fallopian tubes). The only exception to this general rule is sometimes made for young women with Stage IA and IB cancers who have not had all the children they want.

Surgeons may also remove the appendix and the omentum, a portion of the lining of the abdomen. There are two reasons for removing this structure: (1) it may contain clusters of cancer cells, indicating that what appears to be a Stage I disease is really Stage III, and (2) it may interfere with radiation therapy initiated during surgery. We will discuss this mode of treatment later in this chapter.

Because the surgeon will try to remove as much cancer as possible during the operation, he or she will have to make a vertical incision in the abdomen. The Pfannenstiel (bikini-line) incision used for other types of gynecologic surgery is not appropriate because accurately staging the cancer via such a small incision is difficult, if not impossible.

During the operation, the surgeon will do everything possible to remove all of the cancer. He or she will examine the liver and the small and large intestines for telltale signs of cancer. Samples of tissues that look abnormal will be removed for biopsy, and samples of normal-looking tissue will also be taken—this "blind biopsy" may detect cancer that is not visible to the surgeon's eye. In addition, a saline solution of salt and purified water is used to "wash" the abdomen. When the wash is removed, it will be checked for cancer cells that it has sloughed off.

Second-Look Surgery

In addition to the original operation to diagnose ovarian cancer and remove as much of the cancer and diseased organs as possible, many patients have further surgery to determine whether treatment has worked. This operation usually is performed after chemotherapy has been completed and appears to have succeeded in eradicating the cancer. "Second-look" surgery is regarded as the only way to learn for sure whether or not a patient is free of disease. If not disease-free, she will need more chemotherapy.

The second-look operation is major surgery. It takes one to four hours and requires at least a six-day hospital stay. The surgeon checks the abdomen and pelvis for signs of cancer, takes tissue samples for biopsy, and washes the abdomen with fluid that will once again be examined for cancer cells.

In about half of all cases, the second look finds cancer that could not have been detected otherwise. And about one-third of all women whose second looks reveal no sign of cancer eventually will develop a recurrence. For these reasons, some physicians have questioned the value of the second look. They argue that the surgery presents a number of medical risks that cannot be justified since no good treatment exists for patients whose disease has not responded to chemotherapy. Instead of a second look, these critics of the surgery advocate continuing chemotherapy. However, this remains a minority view and "second look" surgery continues to be recommended for most patients.

RADIATION

Radiation therapy usually is recommended only for Stages I and II ovarian cancer. Such treatment often involves injecting a liquid containing radioactive phosphorus—a substance called P32—into the pelvic and abdominal cavities. This is called intraperitoneal radiotherapy. The liquid coats these areas and kills the cancer cells. In some studies the five-year survival rate for women with Stage I ovarian cancer treated with P32 is 85–90 percent. As an alternative to P32, radiation can be delivered to the target areas via a beam from an X-ray machine. Sometimes chemotherapy instead of P32 may be recommended for women with Stages I and II ovarian cancer.

CHEMOTHERAPY

A number of different chemotherapeutic agents are used to treat ovarian cancer. Although either chemotherapy or P32 may be recommended for Stage I and II cases, radiation therapy is not considered effective for more advanced Stage III and IV cancers. These are treated with a combination of drugs, most of which include a drug called cisplatin (Platinol). When chemotherapy is used for Stage II ovarian cancer, the combination most often recommended is cyclophosphamide and cisplatin. Other possible combinations:

- Cyclophosphamide, doxorubicin, and cisplatin
- Cyclophosphamide, hexamethylmelamine, doxorubicin, and cisplatin
- Doxorubicin and cisplatin

A number of new drugs are being studied. Taxol, a drug made from the bark of the Pacific yew tree, shows great promise. In studies so far it has produced remissions in 30–35 percent of women with recurrent ovarian cancer. This does not represent a cure—in most cases the cancer returned. But taxol's anticancer effects are so striking that it may yet yield a more effective treatment. Unfortunately, supplies are limited. It takes the bark of six 100-year-old yews to produce enough taxol to treat one patient. Researchers are attempting to synthesize taxol in the laboratory but have not yet succeeded.

Researchers are also exploring the use of monoclonal antibodies, substances made in the laboratory, that can locate and attach themselves to cancer cells. If monoclonal antibodies can be fused with substances capable of killing cancer cells, they could be used like "smart bombs" to deliver a lethal dose of cancer-killing substance directly to tumor cells.

CLINICAL TRIALS

In addition to today's standard treatments for ovarian and breast cancer, patients can choose to participate in studies aimed at evaluating new and promising approaches. These ongoing studies, called clinical trials, or protocols, seek to determine whether new types of treatment are as effective or more effective than the drugs, radiation, and even the surgery usually employed to treat different types of cancer.

When a new drug or other mode of treatment shows promise in laboratory studies, the next step is to see if it works on patients. Initially, a new drug would be offered only to people with advanced cancer who have little to lose by trying something new. It might turn out to be the miracle that saves their lives. Obviously, these new treatment approaches are very carefully thought out before being offered to humans, no matter how sick they are. Before asking for human volunteers to test a new drug, researchers must be pretty sure that the substance won't do more harm than good, although they can never be positive that humans will respond as well as, say, laboratory mice.

The first studies of a new drug in humans, called phase I protocols, are designed to determine what dosages are safe and what side effects occur with what severity.

If the phase I studies are successful, researchers move on to phase II to find out how effective the drugs are against different types of cancer. Usually people offered the opportunity to participate in phase II trials have recurrent but not immediately life-threatening cancer. Next come phase III trials to compare the new drug with the ones in current use.

Participation in clinical trials is strictly voluntary. Some doctors encourage their patients to take part; others are less enthusiastic. This seeming reluctance may stem from a physician's doubts about the efficacy of the new method.

Or the doctor may not have the time to fill out all the forms and do all the extra work involved in clinical trials.

If you do decide to participate in a clinical trial and find that the treatment isn't helping, or that you can't tolerate the side effects, or that all the checkups required are too inconvenient—for any reason at all really—you are free to withdraw at any time. The advantage of participating is that you may be among the first to get the benefits of a promising new treatment. The disadvantage is that the new treatment may not work as well as standard approaches, although by the time a new mode of treatment gets to a phase-three clinical trial researchers usually have very good reason to expect it to be better than, not just equal to, standard treatment.

If you do decide to participate, you will be asked to sign an "informed consent" document much like the form you sign authorizing a doctor to perform surgery. You should thoroughly understand the risks and potential benefits of taking part in the study. Don't sign unless all of your questions have been answered to your satisfaction.

Clinical trials are immensely important. Without them, treatment would improve slowly, if at all. Your doctor has access to a National Cancer Institute computer program called Physicians Data Query (PDQ), which supplies up-to-date information on all clinical trials in progress for all types of cancer. You can get information yourself by calling the NCI's toll-free number: (800) 4-CANCER.

YOU now have all of the information you need to deal with your risk of breast or ovarian cancer. You know what preventive measures you can take and what you can do to detect either disease as early as possible. Unless your risk is particularly high, none of these measures is any different from those recommended for women whose risks are normal.

By reading this book you have taken an important step

toward protecting your health. You have armed yourself with facts and confronted your fears. Now it is time to put your worries aside and concentrate on beating the odds. In all likelihood, you now know that they are not as formidable as you supposed.

Appendixes

Appendix 1: Fat and Calorie Tables

Meats

Product (3½ ounces cooked)[1]	Saturated Fatty Acids (grams)	Cholesterol (milligrams)	Total Fat[2] (grams)	Calories from Fat[3] (%)	Total Calories
Beef					
Kidneys, simmered[2]	1.1	387	3.4	21	144
Liver, braised[2]	1.9	389	4.9	27	161
Round, top round, lean only, broiled	2.2	84	6.2	29	191
Round, eye of round, lean only, roasted	2.5	69	6.5	32	183
Round, tip round, lean only, roasted	2.8	81	7.5	36	190
Round, full cut, lean only, choice, broiled	2.9	82	8.0	37	194
Round, bottom round, lean only, braised	3.4	96	9.7	39	222
Short loin, top loin, lean only, broiled	3.6	76	8.9	40	203

1. 3½ ozs = 100 grams (approximately)
2. Total fat = saturated fatty acids plus monounsaturated fatty acids plus polyunsaturated fatty acids.
3. Percent calories from fat = (total fat calories divided by total calories) multiplied by 100; total fat calories = total fat (grams) multiplied by 9.
4. — = Information not available in sources used.
Source: National Heart, Lung, and Blood Institute.

Product (3½ ounces cooked)[1]	Saturated Fatty Acids (grams)	Cholesterol (milligrams)	Total Fat[2] (grams)	Calories from Fat[3] (%)	Total Calories
Wedge-bone sirloin, lean only, broiled	3.6	89	8.7	38	208
Short loin, tenderloin, lean only, broiled	3.6	84	9.3	41	204
Chuck, arm pot roast, lean only, braised	3.8	101	10.0	39	231
Short loin, T-bone steak, lean only, choice, broiled	4.2	80	10.4	44	214
Short loin, porterhouse steak, lean only, choice, broiled	4.3	80	10.8	45	218
Brisket, whole, lean only, braised	4.6	93	12.8	48	241
Rib eye, small end (ribs 10–12), lean only, choice, broiled	4.9	80	11.6	47	225
Rib, whole (ribs 6–12), lean only, roasted	5.8	81	13.8	52	240
Flank, lean only, choice, braised	5.9	71	13.8	51	244
Rib, large end (ribs 6–9), lean only, broiled	6.1	82	14.2	55	233
Chuck, blade roast, lean only, braised	6.2	106	15.3	51	270
Corned beef, cured, brisket, cooked	6.3	98	19.0	68	251

Product (3½ ounces cooked)[1]	Saturated Fatty Acids (grams)	Cholesterol (milligrams)	Total Fat[2] (grams)	Calories from Fat[3] (%)	Total Calories
Flank, lean and fat, choice, braised	6.6	72	15.5	54	257
Ground, lean, broiled medium	7.2	87	18.5	61	272
Round, full cut, lean and fat, choice, braised	7.3	84	18.2	60	274
Rib, short ribs, lean only, choice, braised	7.7	93	18.1	55	295
Short loin, T-bone steak, lean and fat, choice, broiled	10.2	84	24.6	68	324
Chuck, arm pot roast, lean and fat, braised	10.7	99	26.0	67	350
Salami, cured, cooked, smoked, 3–4 slices	9.0	65	20.7	71	262
Sausage, cured, cooked, smoked, about 2	11.4	67	26.9	78	312
Bologna, cured, 3–4 slices	12.1	58	28.5	82	312
Frankfurter, cured, about 2	12.0	61	28.5	82	315
Lamb					
Leg, lean only, roasted	3.0	89	8.2	39	191
Loin chop, lean only, broiled	4.1	94	9.4	39	215
Rib, lean only, roasted	5.7	88	12.3	48	232
Arm chop, lean only, braised	6.0	122	14.6	47	279

Product (3½ ounces cooked)[1]	Saturated Fatty Acids (grams)	Cholesterol (milligrams)	Total Fat[2] (grams)	Calories from Fat[3] (%)	Total Calories
Rib, lean and fat, roasted	14.2	90	30.6	75	368
Pork					
Cured, ham steak, boneless, extra lean, unheated	1.4	45	4.2	31	122
Liver, braised[2]	1.4	355	4.4	24	165
Kidneys, braised[2]	1.5	480	4.7	28	161
Fresh, loin, tenderloin, lean only, roasted	1.7	93	4.8	26	166
Cured, shoulder, arm picnic, lean only, roasted	2.4	48	7.0	37	170
Cured, ham, boneless, regular, roasted	3.1	59	9.0	46	178
Fresh, leg (ham), shank half, lean only, roasted	3.6	92	10.5	44	215
Fresh, leg (ham), rump half, lean only, roasted	3.7	96	10.7	43	221
Fresh, loin, center loin, sirloin, lean only, roasted	4.5	91	13.1	49	240
Fresh loin, sirloin, lean only, roasted	4.5	90	13.2	50	236
Fresh, loin, center rib, lean only, roasted	4.8	79	13.8	51	245

Product (3½ ounces cooked)[1]	Saturated Fatty Acids (grams)	Cholesterol (milligrams)	Total Fat[2] (grams)	Calories from Fat[3] (%)	Total Calories
Fresh, loin, top loin, lean only, roasted	4.8	79	13.8	51	245
Fresh, shoulder, blade, Boston, lean only, roasted	5.8	98	16.8	59	256
Fresh, loin, blade, lean only, roasted	6.6	89	19.3	62	279
Fresh, loin, sirloin, lean and fat, roasted	7.4	91	20.4	63	291
Cured, shoulder, arm picnic, lean and fat, roasted	7.7	58	21.4	69	280
Fresh, loin, center loin, lean and fat, roasted	7.9	91	21.8	64	305
Cured, shoulder, blade roll, lean and fat, roasted	8.4	67	23.5	74	287
Italian sausage, fresh, cooked	9.0	78	25.7	72	323
Bratwurst, fresh, cooked	9.3	60	25.9	77	301
Chitterlings, fresh, cooked	10.1	143	28.8	86	303
Liver sausage, cured, liverwurst	10.6	158	28.5	79	326
Smoked link sausage, cured, grilled	11.3	68	31.8	74	389
Spareribs, fresh, lean and fat, braised	11.8	121	30.3	69	397

Product (3½ ounces cooked)[1]	Saturated Fatty Acids (grams)	Cholesterol (milligrams)	Total Fat[2] (grams)	Calories from Fat[3] (%)	Total Calories
Salami, cured, dry or hard	11.9	—[4]	33.7	75	407
Bacon, fried	17.4	85	49.2	78	576
Veal					
Rump, lean only, roasted	—	128	2.2	13	156
Sirloin, lean only, roasted	—	128	3.2	19	153
Arm steak, lean only, cooked	—	90	5.3	24	200
Loin chop, lean only, cooked	—	90	6.7	29	207
Blade, lean only, cooked	—	90	7.8	33	211
Cutlet, medium fat, braised or broiled	4.8	128	11.0	37	271
Foreshank, medium fat, stewed	—	90	10.4	43	216
Plate, medium fat, stewed	—	90	21.2	63	303
Rib, medium fat, roasted	7.1	128	16.9	70	218
Flank, medium fat, stewed	—	90	32.3	75	390

Poultry

Turkey, fryer-roasters, light meat without skin, roasted	0.4	86	1.9	8	140
Chicken, roasters, light meat without skin, roasted	1.1	75	4.1	24	153
Turkey, fryer-roasters, light meat with skin, roasted	1.3	95	4.6	25	164

Product (3½ ounces cooked)[1]	Saturated Fatty Acids (grams)	Cholesterol (milligrams)	Total Fat[2] (grams)	Calories from Fat[3] (%)	Total Calories
Chicken, broilers or fryers, light meat without skin, roasted	1.3	85	4.5	24	173
Turkey, fryer-roasters, dark meat without skin, roasted	1.4	112	4.3	24	162
Chicken, stewing, light meat without skin, stewed	2.0	70	8.0	34	213
Turkey roll, light and dark	2.0	55	7.0	42	149
Turkey, fryer-roasters, dark meat with skin, roasted	2.1	117	7.1	35	182
Chicken, roasters, dark meat without skin, roasted	2.4	75	8.8	44	178
Chicken, broilers or fryers, dark meat without skin, roasted	2.7	93	9.7	43	205
Chicken, broilers or fryers, light meat with skin, roasted	3.0	85	10.9	44	222
Chicken, stewing, dark meat without skin, stewed	4.1	95	15.3	53	258
Chicken, broilers or fryers, dark meat with skin, roasted	4.4	91	15.8	56	253

Product (3½ ounces cooked)[1]	Saturated Fatty Acids (grams)	Cholesterol (milligrams)	Total Fat[2] (grams)	Calories from Fat[3] (%)	Total Calories
Duck, domesticated, flesh only, roasted	4.2	89	11.2	50	201
Goose, domesticated, flesh only, roasted	4.6	96	12.7	48	238
Turkey bologna, about 3½ slices	5.1	99	15.2	69	199
Chicken frankfurter, about 2	5.5	101	19.5	68	257
Turkey frankfurter, about 2	5.9	107	17.7	70	226

Fish and Shellfish

Product (3½ ounces cooked)[1]	Saturated Fatty Acids (grams)	Cholesterol (milligrams)	Omega-3 Fatty Acids (grams)	Total Fat[2] (grams)	Calories From Fat[3] (%)	Total Calories
Finfish						
Haddock, dry heat	0.2	74	0.2	0.9	7	112
Cod, Atlantic, dry heat	0.2	55	0.2	0.9	7	105
Pollock, walleye, dry heat	0.2	96	1.5	1.1	9	113
Perch, mixed species, dry heat	0.2	42	0.3	1.2	9	117
Grouper, mixed species, dry heat	0.3	47	—	1.3	10	118

Product (3½ ounces cooked)[1]	Saturated Fatty Acids (grams)	Choles-terol (milli-grams)	Omega-3 Fatty Acids (grams)	Total Fat[2] (grams)	Calories From Fat[3] (%)	Total Calories
Whiting, mixed species, dry heat	0.3	84	0.9	1.7	13	115
Snapper, mixed species, dry heat	0.4	47	—	1.7	12	128
Halibut, Atlantic and Pacific, dry heat	0.4	41	0.6	2.9	19	140
Rockfish, Pacific, dry heat	0.5	44	0.5	2.0	15	121
Sea bass, mixed species, dry heat	0.7	53	—	2.5	19	124
Trout, rainbow, dry heat	0.8	73	0.9	4.3	26	151
Swordfish, dry heat	1.4	50	1.1	5.1	30	155
Tuna, bluefin, dry heat	1.6	49	—	6.3	31	184
Salmon, sockeye, dry heat	1.9	87	1.3	11.0	46	216
Anchovy, European, canned	2.2	—	2.1	9.7	42	210
Herring, Atlantic, dry heat	2.6	77	2.1	11.5	51	203
Eel, dry heat	3.0	161	0.7	15.0	57	236
Mackerel, Atlantic, dry heat	4.2	75	1.3	17.8	61	262
Pompano, Florida, dry heat	4.5	64	—	12.1	52	211

Product (3½ ounces cooked)[1]	Saturated Fatty Acids (grams)	Choles-terol (milli-grams)	Omega-3 Fatty Acids (grams)	Total Fat[2] (grams)	Calories From Fat[3] (%)	Total Calories
Crustaceans						
Lobster, northern	0.1	72	0.1	0.6	6	98
Crab, blue, moist heat	0.2	100	0.5	1.8	16	102
Shrimp, mixed species, moist heat	0.3	195	0.3	1.1	10	99
Mollusks						
Whelk, moist heat	0.1	130	—	0.8	3	275
Clam, mixed species, moist heat	0.2	67	0.3	2.0	12	148
Mussel, blue, moist heat	0.9	56	0.8	4.5	23	172
Oyster, Eastern, moist heat	1.3	109	1.0	5.0	33	137

Dairy and Egg Products

Product	Saturated Fat (grams)	Cholesterol (milligrams)	Total Fat[2] (grams)	Calories from Fat[3] (%)	Total Calories
Milk (8 oz.)					
Skim milk	0.3	4	0.4	5	86
Buttermilk	1.3	9	2.2	20	99
Low-fat milk, 1% fat	1.6	10	2.6	23	102
Low-fat milk, 2% fat	2.9	18	4.7	35	121
Whole milk, 3.3% fat	5.1	33	8.2	49	150
Yogurt (4 oz.)					
Plain yogurt, low-fat	0.1	2	0.2	3	63

Product	Saturated Fat (grams)	Cholesterol (milligrams)	Total Fat[2] (grams)	Calories from Fat[3] (%)	Total Calories
Plain yogurt	2.4	14	3.7	47	70
Cheese					
Cottage cheese, low-fat, 1% fat, 4 oz.	0.7	5	1.2	13	82
Mozzarella, part-skim, 1 oz.	2.9	16	4.5	56	72
Cottage cheese, creamed, 4 oz.	3.2	17	5.1	39	117
Mozzarella, 1 oz.	3.7	22	6.1	69	80
Sour cream, 1 oz.	3.7	12	5.9	87	61
American processed cheese spread, pasteurized, 1 oz.	3.8	16	6.0	66	82
Feta, 1 oz.	4.2	25	6.0	72	75
Neufchatel, 1 oz.	4.2	22	6.6	81	74
Camembert, 1 oz.	4.3	20	6.9	73	85
American processed cheese food, pasteurized, 1 oz.	4.4	18	7.0	68	93
Provolone, 1 oz.	4.8	20	7.6	68	100
Limburger, 1 oz.	4.8	26	7.7	75	93
Brie, 1 oz.	4.9	28	7.9	74	95
Romano, 1 oz.	4.9	29	7.6	63	110
Gouda, 1 oz.	5.0	32	7.8	69	101
Swiss, 1 oz.	5.0	26	7.8	65	107
Edam, 1 oz.	5.0	25	7.9	70	101
Brick, 1 oz.	5.3	27	8.4	72	105
Blue, 1 oz.	5.3	21	8.2	73	100
Gruyere, 1 oz.	5.4	31	9.2	71	117
Muenster, 1 oz.	5.4	27	8.5	74	104
Parmesan, 1 oz.	5.4	22	8.5	59	129
Monterey Jack, 1 oz.	5.5	25	8.6	73	106
Roquefort, 1 oz.	5.5	26	8.7	75	105

Product	Saturated Fat (grams)	Cholesterol (milligrams)	Total Fat[2] (grams)	Calories from Fat[3] (%)	Total Calories
Ricotta, part-skim, 4 oz.	5.6	25	9.0	52	156
American processed cheese, pasteurized, 1 oz.	5.6	27	8.9	75	106
Colby, 1 oz.	5.7	27	9.1	73	112
Cheddar, 1 oz.	6.0	30	9.4	74	114
Cream cheese, 1 oz.	6.2	31	9.9	90	99
Ricotta, whole milk, 4 oz.	9.4	58	14.7	67	197
Eggs					
Egg, chicken, white	0	0	trace	0	16
Egg, chicken, whole	1.7	274	5.6	64	79
Egg, chicken, yolk	1.7	272	5.6	80	63

Frozen Desserts

Product (1 cup)	Saturated Fatty Acids (grams)	Cholesterol (milligrams)	Total Fat[2] (grams)	Calories from Fat[3] (%)	Total Calories
Fruit popsicle, 1 bar	—	—	0.0	0	65
Fruit ice	—	—	trace	0	247
Fudgsicle	—	—	0.2	2	91
Frozen yogurt, fruit-flavored	—	—	2.0	8	216
Sherbet, orange	2.4	14	3.8	13	270
Pudding pops, 1 pop	2.5	1	2.6	25	94
Ice milk, vanilla, soft-serve	2.9	13	4.6	19	223
Ice milk, vanilla, hard	3.5	18	5.6	28	184

Product (1 cup)	Saturated Fatty Acids (grams)	Cholesterol (milligrams)	Total Fat[2] (grams)	Calories from Fat[3] (%)	Total Calories
Ice cream, vanilla, regular	8.9	59	14.3	48	269
Ice cream, French vanilla, soft-serve	13.5	153	22.5	54	377
Ice cream, vanilla, rich, 16% fat	14.7	88	23.7	61	349

Fats and Oils

Product (1 Tbsp.)	Saturated Fatty Acids (grams)	Cholesterol (milligrams)	Polyunsaturated Fatty Acids (grams)	Monounsaturated Fatty Acids (grams)
Rapeseed oil (canola oil)	0.9	0	4.5	7.6
Safflower oil	1.2	0	10.1	1.6
Sunflower oil	1.4	0	5.5	6.2
Peanut butter, smooth	1.5	0	2.3	3.7
Corn oil	1.7	0	8.0	3.3
Olive oil	1.8	0	1.1	9.9
Hydrogenated sunflower oil	1.8	0	4.9	6.3
Margarine, liquid, bottled	1.8	0	5.1	3.9
Margarine, soft, tub	1.8	0	3.9	4.8
Sesame oil	1.9	0	5.7	5.4
Soybean oil	2.0	0	7.9	3.2
Margarine, stick	2.1	0	3.6	5.1
Peanut oil	2.3	0	4.3	6.2
Cottonseed oil	3.5	0	7.1	2.4
Lard	5.0	12	1.4	5.8
Beef tallow	6.4	14	0.5	5.3
Palm oil	6.7	0	1.3	5.0

Product (1 Tbsp.)	Saturated Fatty Acids (grams)	Cholesterol (milligrams)	Polyunsaturated Fatty Acids (grams)	Monounsaturated Fatty Acids (grams)
Butter	7.1	31	0.4	3.3
Cocoa butter	8.1	0	0.4	4.5
Palm kernel oil	11.1	0	0.2	1.5
Coconut oil	11.8	0	0.2	0.8

Nuts and Seeds

Product (1 oz.)	Saturated Fatty Acids (grams)	Cholesterol (milligrams)	Total Fat[2] (grams)	Calories from Fat[3] (%)	Total Calories
European chestnuts	0.2	0	1.1	9	105
Filberts or hazelnuts	1.3	0	17.8	89	179
Almonds	1.4	0	15.0	80	167
Pecans	1.5	0	18.4	89	187
Sunflower seed kernels, roasted	1.5	0	1.4	77	165
English walnuts	1.6	0	17.6	87	182
Pistachio nuts	1.7	0	13.7	75	164
Peanuts	1.9	0	14.0	76	164
Hickory nuts	2.0	0	18.3	88	187
Pine nuts, pignolia	2.2	0	14.4	89	146
Pumpkin and squash seed kernels	2.3	0	12.0	73	148
Cashew nuts	2.6	0	13.2	73	163
Macadamia nuts	3.1	0	20.9	95	199
Brazil nuts	4.6	0	18.8	91	186
Coconut meat, unsweetened	16.3	0	18.3	88	187

Breads, Cereals, Pasta, Rice, and Dried Peas and Beans

Product	Saturated Fatty Acids (grams)	Cholesterol (milligrams)	Total Fat[2] (grams)	Calories from Fat[3] (%)	Total Calories
Breads					
Melba toast, 1 plain	0.1	0	trace	0	20
Pita, ½ large shell	0.1	0	1.0	5	165
Corn tortilla	0.1	0	1.0	14	65
Rye bread, 1 slice	0.2	0	1.0	14	65
English muffin	0.3	0	1.0	6	140
Bagel, 1, 3½″ diameter	0.3	0	2.0	9	200
White bread, 1 slice	0.3	0	1.0	14	65
Rye krisp, 2 triple crackers	0.3	0	1.0	16	56
Whole-wheat bread, 1 slice	0.4	0	1.0	13	70
Saltines, 4	0.5	4	1.0	18	50
Hamburger bun	0.5	trace	2.0	16	115
Hot dog bun	0.5	trace	2.0	16	115
Pancake, 1, 4″ diameter	0.5	16	2.0	30	60
Bran muffin, 1, 2½″ diameter	1.4	24	6.0	43	125
Corn muffin, 1, 2½″ diameter	1.5	23	5.0	31	145
Plain doughnut, 1, 3¼″ diameter	2.8	20	12.0	51	210
Croissant, 1, 4½″ by 4″	3.5	13	12.0	46	235
Waffle, 1, 7″ diameter	4.0	102	13.0	48	245
Cereals (1 cup)					
Corn flakes	trace	—	0.1	0	98

Product	Saturated Fatty Acids (grams)	Cholesterol (milligrams)	Total Fat[2] (grams)	Calories from Fat[3] (%)	Total Calories
Cream of wheat, cooked	trace	—	0.5	3	134
Corn grits, cooked	trace	—	0.5	3	146
Oatmeal, cooked	0.4	—	2.4	15	145
Granola	5.8	—	33.1	50	595
100% Natural Cereal with raisins and dates	13.7	—	20.3	37	496
Pasta (1 cup)					
Spaghetti, cooked	0.1	0	1.0	6	155
Elbow macaroni, cooked	0.1	0	1.0	6	155
Egg noodles, cooked	0.5	50	2.0	11	160
Chow mein noodles, canned	2.1	5	11.0	45	220
Rice (1 cup cooked)					
Rice, white	0.1	0	0.5	2	225
Rice, brown	0.3	0	1.0	4	230
Dried Peas and Beans (1 cup cooked)					
Split peas	0.1	0	0.8	3	231
Kidney beans	0.1	0	1.0	4	225
Lima beans	0.2	0	0.7	3	217
Black-eyed peas	0.3	0	1.2	5	200
Chick-peas	0.4	0	4.3	14	269

Sweets and Snacks

Beverages

Product	Saturated Fatty Acids	Cholesterol	Total Fat	Calories from Fat	Total Calories
Ginger ale, 12 oz.	0.0	0	0.0	0	125
Cola, regular, 12 oz.	0.0	0	0.0	0	160

Product	Saturated Fatty Acids (grams)	Cholesterol (milligrams)	Total Fat[2] (grams)	Calories from Fat[3] (%)	Total Calories
Chocolate shake, 10 oz.	6.5	37	10.5	26	360
Candy (1 oz.)					
Hard candy	0.0	0	0.0	0	110
Gumdrops	trace	0	trace	trace	100
Fudge	2.1	1	3.0	24	115
Milk chocolate, plain	5.4	6	9.0	56	145
Cookies					
Vanilla wafers, 5, 1¾″ diameter	0.9	12	3.3	32	94
Fig bars, 4, 1⅝″ by 1⅝″ by ⅜″	1.0	27	4.0	17	210
Chocolate brownie with icing, 1½″ by 1¾″ by ⅞″	1.6	14	4.0	36	100
Oatmeal cookies, 4, 2⅝″ diameter	2.5	2	10.0	37	245
Chocolate chip cookies, 4, 2¼″ diameter	3.9	18	11.0	54	185
Cakes and Pies					
Angel food cake, 1/12 of 10″ cake	trace	0	trace	trace	125
Gingerbread, 1/9 of 8″ cake	1.1	1	4.0	21	175
White layer cake with white icing, 1/16 of 9″ cake	2.1	3	9.0	32	260
Yellow layer cake with chocolate icing, 1/16 of 9″ cake	3.0	36	8.0	31	235
Pound cake, 1/17 of loaf	3.0	64	5.0	41	110

Product	Saturated Fatty Acids (grams)	Cholesterol (milligrams)	Total Fat[2] (grams)	Calories from Fat[3] (%)	Total Calories
Devil's food cake with chocolate icing, 1/16 of 9″ cake	3.5	37	8.0	31	235
Lemon meringue pie, 1/6 of 9″ pie	4.3	143	14.0	36	355
Apple pie, 1/6 of 9″ pie	4.6	0	18.0	40	405
Cream pie, 1/6 of 9″ pie	15.0	8	23.0	46	455
Snacks					
Popcorn, air-popped, 1 cup	trace	0	trace	trace	30
Pretzels, stick, 2¼″, 10 pretzels	trace	0	trace	trace	10
Popcorn with oil and salted, 1 cup	0.5	0	3.0	49	55
Corn chips, 1 oz.	1.4	25	9.0	52	155
Potato chips, 1 oz.	2.6	0	10.1	62	147
Pudding					
Gelatin, ½ cup	0.0	0	0.0	0	70
Tapioca, ½ cup	2.3	15	4.0	25	145
Chocolate pudding, ½ cup	2.4	15	4.0	24	150

Miscellaneous

Gravies (½ cup)

Au jus, canned	0.1	1	0.3	3	80
Turkey, canned	0.7	3	2.5	37	61

Product	Saturated Fatty Acids (grams)	Cholesterol (milligrams)	Total Fat[2] (grams)	Calories from Fat[3] (%)	Total Calories
Beef, canned	1.4	4	2.8	41	62
Chicken, canned	1.7	3	6.8	65	95
Sauces (½ cup)					
Sweet and sour	trace	0	0.1	<1	147
Barbecue	0.3	0	2.3	22	94
White	3.2	17	6.7	50	121
Cheese	4.7	26	8.6	50	154
Sour cream	8.5	45	15.1	53	255
Hollandaise	20.9	94	34.1	87	353
Bearnaise	20.9	99	34.1	88	351
Salad Dressings (1 Tbsp.)					
Russian, low-calorie	0.1	1	0.7	27	23
French, low-calorie	0.1	1	0.9	37	22
Italian, low-calorie	0.2	1	1.5	85	16
Thousand Island, low-calorie	0.2	2	1.6	59	24
Imitation mayonnaise	0.5	4	2.9	75	35
Thousand Island, regular	0.9	—	5.6	86	59
Italian, regular	1.0	—	7.1	93	69
Russian, regular	1.1	—	7.8	92	76
French, regular	1.5	—	6.4	86	67
Blue cheese	1.5	—	8.0	93	77
Mayonnaise	1.6	8	11.0	100	99
Other					
Olives, green, 4 medium	0.2	0	1.5	90	15
Nondairy creamer, powdered, 1 tsp.	0.7	0	1.0	90	10

Product	Saturated Fatty Acids (grams)	Cholesterol (milligrams)	Total Fat[2] (grams)	Calories from Fat[3] (%)	Total Calories
Avocado, Florida	5.3	0	27.0	72	340
Pizza, cheese, 1/8 of 15″ pie	4.1	56	9.0	28	290
Quiche lorraine, 1/8 of 8″ pie	23.2	285	48.0	72	600

Appendix 2: A Day of Low-Fat Meals

Breakfast

1 cup shredded wheat with peach slices
1 cup 1% milk
1 slice whole-wheat toast with 1 teaspoon margarine
1 cup pink grapefruit juice
black coffee

Snack

1 toasted English muffin with 1 tsp. margarine

Lunch

3 oz. turkey salad on lettuce with tomato wedges
1 thick slice of French bread
10 animal crackers
tea with lemon

Snack

1 banana

Dinner

3 oz. broiled halibut with lemon and herb seasoning
½ cup brown rice with mushrooms
1 dinner roll with 1 tsp. margarine
¾ cup carrot strips with 1 tsp. margarine
spinach salad with 1 Tbsp. oil and vinegar dressing
1 cup 1% milk
1 small piece homemade yellow cake*

Nutrient Analysis

Total calories	2000
Total fat (percent of calories)	30
Saturated fat (percent of calories)	10
Cholesterol	172 mg

*Homemade desserts should be made with unsaturated fats instead of saturated fats. Two egg whites may be substituted for one egg yolk.
Source: National Heart, Lung, and Blood Institute

Appendix 3: A Guide to Choosing Low-Fat Foods

Following a low-saturated fat, low-cholesterol diet is a balancing act: getting the variety of foods necessary to supply the nutrients you need without too much saturated fat and cholesterol or excess calories. One way to assure variety—and with it, a well-balanced diet—is to select foods each day from each

Foods	Choose
Meat, Poultry, Fish and Shellfish (up to 6 oz. a day)	Lean cuts of meat with fat trimmed, such as: Beef, round, sirloin, chuck, loin Lamb, leg, arm, loin, rib Pork, tenderloin, leg (fresh), shoulder (arm or picnic) Veal, all trimmed cuts except ground Poultry without skin Fish Shellfish
Dairy Products (2 servings a day; 3 servings for women who are pregnant or breast-feeding)	Skim milk, 1% milk, low-fat buttermilk, low-fat evaporated or nonfat milk Low-fat yogurt Low-fat soft cheeses, such as cottage, farmer, pot Cheeses labeled no more than 2–6 gm. of fat an oz.
Eggs (no more than 3 egg yolks a week	Egg whites Cholesterol-free egg substitutes

of the following food groups. How many portions and the size of each portion should be adjusted to reach and maintain your desirable weight. As a guide, the recommended daily number of portions is listed for each food group.

Go Easy on	Decrease
	"Prime" grade
	Fatty cuts of meat, such as:
	Beef, corned beef brisket, regular ground, short ribs
	Pork, spareribs, blade roll, fresh
	Goose, domestic duck
	Organ meats
	Sausage, bacon
	Regular luncheon meats
	Frankfurters
	Caviar, roe
2% milk	Whole milk, such as regular, evaporated, condensed
Yogurt	
Part-skim ricotta	Cream, half-and-half, most non-dairy creamers, imitation milk products, whipped cream
Part-skim or imitation hard cheese, such as part-skim mozzarella	
	Custard-style yogurt
	Whole-milk ricotta
"Light" cream cheese	Neufchatel
"Light" sour cream	Brie
	Hard cheeses, such as swiss, American, mozzarella, feta, cheddar, muenster
	Cream cheese
	Sour cream
	Egg yolks

Foods	Choose
Fats and Oils (up to 6–8 tsps. a day)	Unsaturated vegetable oils: corn, olive, peanut, rapeseed (canola oil), safflower, sesame, soybean Margarine, or shortening made from unsaturated fats listed above: liquid, tub, stick, diet
Breads, Cereals, Pasta, Rice, Dried Peas and Beans (6–11 servings a day)	Breads, such as white, whole-wheat, pumpernickel, rye, pita; bagels; English muffins; sandwich buns; dinner rolls; rice cakes Low-fat crackers, such as matzo, bread sticks, rye krisp, saltines, zwieback Hot cereals, most cold dry cereals Pasta, such as plain noodles, spaghetti, macaroni Any grain rice Dried peas and beans, such as split peas, black-eyed peas, chick-peas, kidney beans, navy beans, lentils, soybeans, soybean curd (tofu)
Fruits and Vegetables (2–4 servings of fruit and 3–5 servings of vegetables a day)	Fresh, frozen, canned, or dried fruits and vegetables
Sweets and Snacks (avoid too many sweets)	Low-fat frozen desserts, such as sherbet, sorbet, Italian ice, frozen yogurt, popsicles Low-fat cakes, such as angel food cake Low-fat cookies, such as fig bars, gingersnaps

Go Easy on	Decrease
Nuts and seeds Avocados and olives	Butter, coconut oil, palm oil, palm kernel oil, lard, bacon fat Margarine or shortening made from saturated fats listed above
Store-bought pancakes, waffles, biscuits, muffins, cornbread	Croissants, butter rolls, sweet rolls, Danish pastry, doughnuts Most snack crackers, such as cheese crackers, butter crackers, those made with saturated oils Granola-type cereals made with saturated oils Pasta and rice prepared with cream, butter, or cheese sauces; egg noodles
Vegetables prepared in butter, cream, or sauce	
Frozen desserts, such as ice milk	High-fat frozen desserts, such as ice cream, frozen tofu
Homemade cakes, cookies, and pies, using unsaturated oils sparingly	High-fat cakes, such as most store-bought, pound, and frosted cakes
Fruit crisps and cobblers	Store-bought pies Most store-bought cookies

Appendix 4: Desirable Weights for Women
Metropolitan Height and Weight Tables for Women According to Frame, Ages 25–59

Height (in shoes)**		Weight in Pounds (in indoor clothing)*		
Feet	Inches	Small Frame	Medium Frame	Large Frame
4	10	102–111	109–121	118–131
4	11	103–113	111–123	120–134
5	0	104–115	113–126	122–137
5	1	106–118	115–129	125–140
5	2	108–121	118–132	128–143
5	3	111–124	121–135	131–147
5	4	114–127	124–138	134–151
5	5	117–130	127–141	137–155
5	6	120–133	130–144	140–159
5	7	123–136	133–147	143–163
5	8	126–139	136–150	146–167
5	9	129–142	139–153	149–170
5	10	132–145	142–156	152–173
5	11	135–148	145–159	155–176
6	0	138–151	148–162	158–179

*Indoor clothing weighing 3 pounds.
**Shoes with 1-inch heels.
Courtesy Metropolitan Life Insurance Company

Appendix 5: Resources

American Cancer Society (ACS)
1599 Clifton Road, NE
Atlanta, GA 30329
(800) ACS–2345

You can also contact your local ACS office (see Appendix 7 for a list of addresses and telephone numbers), which can provide referrals for mammograms.

The American Cancer Society publishes a wide range of materials about cancer and its prevention and treatment. All are available free of charge. Among them:

- *Nutrition and Cancer: Causes and Prevention*
- *How to Examine Your Breasts*
- *Cancer Facts for Women*
- *Facts on Ovarian Cancer*
- *Helping Children Understand: A Guide for a Parent with Cancer*
- *What Is 'Reach to Recovery'?*
- *After Mastectomy: The Patient Guide*
- *After Mastectomy: The Woman on Her Own*
- *Breast Reconstruction after Mastectomy*
- *Questions and Answers about Pain Control*
- *Sexuality and Cancer*

National Cancer Institute (NCI)
Building 21, Room 10A24
Bethesda, MD 20892
(800) 4–CANCER

NCI publishes a wide range of materials about cancer and its prevention and treatment. All are available free of charge (some are available in Spanish). Among them:

- *Cancer Prevention: Good News, Better News, Best News*
- *Questions and Answers about Breast Lumps*
- *What You Need to Know about Breast Cancer*
- *If You've Thought about Breast Cancer*
- *Cancer of the Ovary*
- *What You Need to Know about Cancer of the Ovary*
- *Breast Biopsy: What You Should Know*
- *Breast Cancer: Understanding Treatment Options*
- *Mastectomy: A Treatment for Breast Cancer*
- *After Breast Cancer: A Guide to Follow-Up Care*
- *When Someone in Your Family Has Cancer*
- *Eating Hints: Recipes and Tips for Better Nutrition during Cancer Treatment*
- *Radiation Therapy and You*
- *Talking with Your Child about Cancer*
- *The Future of Cancer Therapy*
- *What Are Clinical Trials All About?*
- *A Patient's Guide to Research at the Clinical Center*

American College of Radiology (ACR)
1891 Preston White Drive
Reston, VA 22091
(800) ACR–LINE

Accredits mammography facilities nationwide. For a list of accredited facilities in your area, write to the ACR at the above address.

American Society of Plastic and Reconstructive Surgeons
444 East Algonquin Road
Arlington Heights, IL 60005
(800) 635–0635
(312) 228–9900

Provides referrals to plastic surgeons nationwide for breast reconstruction after mastectomy.

Hereditary Cancer Institute
Creighton University
PO Box 3266
Omaha, NE 68103—9990
(800) 648—8133
(402) 280—2942

Evaluates families for evidence of hereditary cancer, identifies high-risk relatives in cancer-prone families, provides recommendations for surveillance or early detection checkups for family members at high risk for cancer, and publishes informational materials for families and physicians.

Gilda Radner Familial Ovarian Cancer Registry
c/o M. Steven Piver, M.D. or Trudy R. Baker, M.D.
Department of Gynecologic Oncology
Roswell Park Cancer Institute
Elm and Carlton Streets
Buffalo, NY 14263
(800) OVARIAN

A national computer tracking system that, as an aid to early detection of ovarian cancer, stores the names of women with two or more close relatives who have been diagnosed with the disease. The registry publishes a newsletter and the brochure *Five Things You Should Know about Ovarian Cancer*.

Susan M. Love, M.D., with Karen Lindsey, DR. SUSAN LOVE'S BREAST BOOK (Reading, MA: Addison-Wesley Publishing Co., 1990, hardcover $18.95, paperback $12.95). A fully comprehensive, authoritative, and reassuring guide to breast cancer and to breast care in general, written by one of the country's leading breast surgeons.

Appendix 6: Cancer Centers

The institutions listed have been recognized as Cancer Centers by the National Cancer Institute. These centers have been rigorously reviewed by the National Cancer Advisory Board. They receive financial support from the National Cancer Institute, the American Cancer Society, and many other sources.

ALABAMA

University of Alabama
Comprehensive Cancer Center*
(205) 934–5077

ARIZONA

University of Arizona
Cancer Center
(602) 626–6044

CALIFORNIA

University of Southern
California
Kenneth Norris, Jr.
Comprehensive Cancer
Center*
(213) 224–6600
University of California at Los
Angeles

Jonsson Comprehensive
Cancer Center*
(213) 825–3181

Drew-Meharry-Morehouse
Consortium Cancer Center
(213) 754–2961

Northern California Cancer
Center
(415) 591–4484

La Jolla Cancer Research
Foundation
(619) 455–6480

University of California at San
Diego
Cancer Center
(619) 534–1501

Beckman Research Institute
City of Hope
(818) 357–9711

Salk Institute
Armand Hammer Center for
Cancer Biology
(619) 453–4100

*Indicates Comprehensive Cancer
Center.
Source: American Cancer Society

California Institute of
  Technology
Cancer Center
(818) 356—6408

COLORADO

University of Colorado Health
  Sciences Center
University of Colorado Cancer
  Center
(303) 270—8801

CONNECTICUT

Yale Comprehensive Cancer
  Center*
(203) 785—4095

DISTRICT OF COLUMBIA

Lombardi Cancer Research
  Center
Georgetown University
  Medical Center
(202) 687—2110

FLORIDA

University of Miami
Sylvester Comprehensive
  Cancer Center*
(305) 548—4800

ILLINOIS

Illinois Cancer Council*
(312) 346—9813
University of Chicago
Cancer Research Center
(312) 702—6180

INDIANA

Purdue University
Cancer Research Center
(317) 494—9129

MAINE

The Jackson Laboratory
(207) 288—3371

MARYLAND

Johns Hopkins Oncology
  Center*
(301) 955—8822

MASSACHUSETTS

Dana-Farber Cancer Institute*
(617) 732—3000

Worcester Foundation for
  Experimental Biology
(508) 842—8921

Massachusetts Institute of
  Technology
Center for Cancer Research
(617) 253—6421

MICHIGAN

Wayne State University
Comprehensive Cancer Center*
(313) 745—8870

University of Michigan
Cancer Center
(313) 936—2516

MINNESOTA

Mayo Comprehensive Cancer
  Center*
(507) 284—4718

NEBRASKA

University of Nebraska
  Medical Center
Eppley Institute
(402) 559—4238

NEW HAMPSHIRE

Dartmouth-Hitchcock Medical
Center
Norris Cotton Cancer Center
(603) 646–5505

NEW YORK

Cold Spring Harbor
Laboratory
(516) 367–8310

Memorial Sloan-Kettering
Cancer Center*
(212) 639–6561

Roswell Park Memorial
Institute*
(716) 845–5770

Albert Einstein College of
Medicine
Cancer Research Center
(212) 430–2302

Columbia University
Cancer Center*
(212) 305–6921

New York University
Cancer Center
(212) 340–5349

University of Rochester
Cancer Center
(716) 275–4911

New York University Medical
Center
Institute of Environmental
Medicine
(212) 340–5280

American Health Foundation
(212) 953–1900

NORTH CAROLINA

Duke Comprehensive Cancer
Center*

(919) 684–3377

University of North Carolina
Lineberger Cancer Research
Center*
(919) 966–3036

Wake Forest University
Bowman Gray School of
Medicine
Cancer Center*
(919) 748–4464

OHIO

Ohio State University
Comprehensive Cancer Center*
(614) 293–3302

Case Western Reserve
University
Ireland Cancer Center
(216) 844–8453

PENNSYLVANIA

Fox Chase Cancer Center*
(215) 728–2781

University of Pennsylvania
Cancer Center
(215) 662–6334

Wistar Institute
(215) 898–3703

Temple University School of
Medicine
Fels Research Institute
(215) 221–4307

University of Pittsburgh
Pittsburgh Cancer Institute*
(412) 647–2072

RHODE ISLAND

Brown University
Roger Williams General
Hospital
(401) 456–2070

TENNESSEE

St. Jude Children's Research
  Hospital
(901) 522-0301

TEXAS

University of Texas
M.D. Anderson Cancer Center*
(713) 792-6000

UTAH

University of Utah Medical
  Center
Utah Regional Cancer Center
(801) 581-8793

VERMONT

University of Vermont
Vermont Regional Cancer
  Center
(802) 656-4414

VIRGINIA

Medical College of Virginia
Massey Cancer Center
(804) 786-9722

University of Virginia
Cancer Center
(804) 924-5111

WASHINGTON

Fred Hutchinson Cancer
  Research Center*
(206) 467-4302

WISCONSIN

University of Wisconsin
Clinical Cancer Center*
(608) 263-8610

University of Wisconsin
McArdle Laboratory for
  Cancer Research
(608) 262-2177

Appendix 7: Chartered Divisions of the American Cancer Society, Inc.

Alabama Division, Inc.

504 Brookwood Boulevard
Homewood, AL 35209
(205) 879–2242

Alaska Division, Inc.

406 West Fireweed Lane
Suite 204
Anchorage, AK 99503
(907) 277–8696

Arizona Division, Inc.

2929 East Thomas Road
Phoenix, AZ 85016
(602) 224–0524

Arkansas Division, Inc.

901 North University
Little Rock, AR 72207
(501) 664–3480

California Division, Inc.

1710 Webster Street
P.O. Box 2061
Oakland, CA 94612
(415) 893–7900

Colorado Division, Inc.

2255 South Oneida
P.O. Box 24669
Denver, CO 80224
(303) 758–2030

Connecticut Division, Inc.

Barnes Park South
14 Village Lane
Wallingford, CT 06492
(203) 265–7161

Delaware Division, Inc.

92 Read's Way
New Castle, DE 19720
(302) 324–4227

District of Columbia Division, Inc.

1825 Connecticut Avenue, NW
Suite 315
Washington, D.C. 20009
(202) 483–2600

Florida Division, Inc.

1001 South MacDill Avenue
Tampa, FL 33629
(813) 253–0541

Georgia Division, Inc.
46 Fifth Street, NE
Atlanta, GA 30308
(404) 892−0026

Hawaii Pacific Division, Inc.
Community Services Center
  Building
200 North Vineyard Boulevard
Honolulu, HI 96817
(808) 531−1662

Idaho Division, Inc.
2676 Vista Avenue
P.O. Bo 5386
Boise, ID 83705
(208) 343−4609

Illinois Division, Inc.
77 East Monroe
Chicago, IL 60603
(312) 641−6150

Indiana Division, Inc.
8730 Commerce Park Place
Indianapolis, IN 46268
(317) 872−4432

Iowa Division, Inc.
8364 Hickman Road, Suite D
Des Moines, IA 50325
(515) 253−0147

Kansas Division, Inc.
1315 SW Arrowhead Road
Topeka, KS 66604
(913) 273−4114

Kentucky Division, Inc.
701 West Muhammad Ali
  Boulevard

P.O. Box 1807
Louisville, KY 40201−1807
(502) 584−6782

Louisiana Division, Inc.
Fidelity Homestead Building
837 Gravier Street
Suite 700
New Orleans, LA 70112−1509
(504) 523−4188

Maine Division, Inc.
52 Federal Street
Brunswick, ME 04011
(207) 729−3339

Maryland Division, Inc.
8219 Town Center Drive
White Marsh, MD 21162−0082
(301) 931−6868

Massachusetts Division, Inc.
247 Commonwealth Avenue
Boston, MA 02116
(617) 267−2650

Michigan Division, Inc.
1205 East Saginaw Street
Lansing, MI 48906
(517) 371−2920

Minnesota Division, Inc.
3316 West 66th Street
Minneapolis, MN 55435
(612) 925−2772

Mississippi Division, Inc.
1380 Livingston Lane
Lakeover Office Park

Jackson, MS 39213
(601) 362–8874

Missouri Division, Inc.
3322 American Avenue
Jefferson City, MO 65102
(314) 893–4800

Montana Division, Inc.
313 N. 32nd Street
Suite 1
Billings, MT 59101
(406) 252–7111

Nebraska Division, Inc.
8502 West Center Road
Omaha, NE 68124–5255
(402) 393–5800

Nevada Division, Inc.
1325 East Harmon
Las Vegas, NV 89119
(702) 798–6857

New Hampshire Division, Inc.
360 Route 101, Unit 501
Bedford, NH 03102–6800
(603) 472–8899

New Jersey Division, Inc.
2600 Route 1, CN 2201
North Brunswick, NJ 08902
(201) 297–8000

New Mexico Division, Inc.
5800 Lomas Boulevard, NE
Albuquerque, NM 87110
(505) 260–2105

New York State Division, Inc.
6725 Lyons Street
P.O. Box 7

East Syracuse, NY 13057
(315) 437–7025

Long Island Division, Inc.
145 Pidgeon Hill Road
Huntington Station, NY 11746
(516) 385–9100

New York City Division, Inc.
19 West 56th Street
New York, NY 10019
(212) 586–8700

Queens Division, Inc.
112–25 Queens Boulevard
Forest Hills, NY 11375
(718) 263–2224

Westchester Division, Inc.
30 Glenn Street
White Plains, NY 10603
(914) 949–4800

North Carolina Division, Inc.
11 South Boylan Avenue
Suite 221
Raleigh, NC 27603
(919) 834–8463

North Dakota Division, Inc.
123 Roberts Street
P.O. Box 426
Fargo, ND 58107
(701) 232–1385

Ohio Division, Inc.
5555 Frantz Road
Dublin, OH 43017
(614) 889–9565

Oklahoma Division, Inc.

3000 United Founders
  Boulevard
Suite 136
Oklahoma City, OK 73112
(405) 843—9888

Oregon Division, Inc.

0330 SW Curry
Portland, OR 97201
(503) 295—6422

Pennsylvania Division, Inc.

Route 422 & Sipe Avenue
P.O. Box 897
Hershey, PA 17033—0897
(717) 533—6144

Philadelphia Division, Inc.

1422 Chestnut Street
Philadelphia, PA 19102
(215) 665—2900

Puerto Rico Division, Inc.

Calle Alverio #577,
Esquina Sargento Medina,
Hato Rey, PR 00918
(809) 764—2295

Rhode Island Division, Inc.

400 Main Street
Pawtucket, RI 02860
(401) 722—8480

South Carolina Division, Inc.

128 Stonemark Lane
Columbia, SC 29210
(803) 750—1693

South Dakota Division, Inc.

4101 Carnegie Place
Sioux Falls, SD 57106—2322
(605) 361—8277

Tennessee Division, Inc.

1315 Eighth Avenue, South
Nashville, TN 37203
(615) 255—1227

Texas Division, Inc.

2433 Ridgepoint Drive
Austin, TX 78754
(512) 928—2262

Utah Division, Inc.

610 East South Temple
Salt Lake City, UT 84102
(801) 322—0431

Vermont Division, Inc.

13 Loomis Street, Drawer C
P.O. Box 1452
Montpelier, VT 05601—1452
(802) 223—2348

Virginia Division, Inc.

4240 Park Place Court
Glen Allen, VA 23060
(804) 270—0142
(800) ACS—2345

Washington Division, Inc.

2120 First Avenue North
Seattle, WA 98109—1140
(206) 283—1152

West Virginia Division, Inc.

2428 Kanawha Boulevard East
Charleston, WV 25311
(304) 344—3611

Wisconsin Division, Inc.
615 North Sherman Avenue
Madison, WI 53704
(608) 249–0487

Wyoming Division, Inc.
2222 House Avenue
Cheyenne, WY 82001
(307) 638–3331

Glossary

Adenocarcinoma: Cancer that originates in gland-forming tissue; breast cancer is an adenocarcinoma.

Adjuvant chemotherapy: Drugs used to treat cancer in addition to surgery and/or radiation.

Alopecia: Hair loss; may occur as a result of chemotherapy.

Alpha-fetoprotein: Blood protein that may indicate the presence of ovarian cancer.

Anesthesia: Loss of sensation due to administration of drugs or gases.

Aneuploid: Cell with an abnormal amount of DNA; aneuploid cancer cells tend to be aggressive.

Animal fat: Dietary fat derived from meats, dairy products, and other animal sources of food; high intake may increase risk of both breast and ovarian cancer.

Antiemetic: Drug to relieve nausea and vomiting.

Anti-oxidant: Substance capable of retarding oxidation and inhibiting action of harmful free radicals in the body See also *Free radicals; Oxidation.*

Areola: Pigmented area surrounding the nipple.

Asbestos: Fire-resistant material; exposure may increase the risk of ovarian cancer.

Ascites: Abdominal fluid; accumulation may cause abdominal swelling.

Aspiration: Drawing fluid out of tissue with a needle and syringe.

Atypical hyperplasia: Abnormalities found in the course of biopsy for benign breast disease that indicate an increased risk of breast cancer. See also *Hyperplasia*.

Autosomal dominant: Pattern of direct genetic transmission from parent to child; applied to cancer, can indicate a 50–50 risk for first-degree relatives of cancer victims.

Axilla: Armpit.

Axillary dissection: Removal of lymph nodes in armpit; sometimes done prior to radiation therapy for breast cancer.

Axillary lymph nodes: Lymph nodes in armpit.

Axillary sampling: Removal of some but not all lymph nodes in armpit prior to radiation therapy for breast cancer.

Barium enema: An X-ray procedure to examine large bowel and urinary tract for growths; sometimes performed when ovarian cancer is suspected.

Benign: Not cancerous.

Biopsy: Surgical procedure to remove tissue for laboratory testing.

Bone scan: A test for bone abnormalities that may indicate breast cancer spread.

CA-125: Substance or "marker" in the blood that may indicate the presence or recurrence of ovarian cancer.

Calcifications: See *Microcalcifications*.

Calorie: Unit of energy derived from food; high-calorie diet may increase cancer risk.

Carcinoembryonic antigen (CEA): Blood test that may indicate presence of cancer.

Carcinogen: Substance capable of causing cancer.

Carcinoma: Cancer arising in skin, glands, and lining of internal organs.

Carcinoma in situ: Cancer that has not spread.

CAT scan: Computerized Axial Tomography; a test sometimes used to examine the liver, lungs, or other organs for cancer spread.

Cathepsin D: Blood protein secreted by cancer cells; the more cathepsin D secreted, the greater the chance of recurrence.

CEA: See *Carcinoembryonic antigen*.

Chemotherapy: Drug treatment for cancer.

Choriocarcinoma: Type of ovarian cancer.

Cisplatin: A drug used to treat ovarian cancer.

Clear cell cystadenocarcinoma: Type of ovarian cancer.

Clinical trial: Study to compare effectiveness of new cancer treatments with standard treatment.

Combination chemotherapy: Use of two or more anticancer drugs.

Combination therapy: More than one form of treatment for cancer; may include surgery plus radiation and/or chemotherapy.

Comedocarcinoma: Type of breast cancer tumor; prognosis is generally favorable.

Control group: Patients receiving standard treatment for comparison with patients receiving new or experimental treatment for cancer in clinical trials (see *Clinical trial*); the term also refers to a group of healthy volunteers who receive no screening or other diagnostic procedures for comparison with a second group who are screened in the course of studies designed to determine whether medical intervention can detect disease at its earliest, most curable stage.

Cyclophosphamide: A drug used to treat both breast and ovarian cancer.

Cyst: Sac that contains fluid; common in the breast.

Cystosarcoma phylloides: Rare type of breast tumor that is often large but usually does not spread.

Cytotoxic: Toxic to cells; drugs used to treat cancer are cytotoxic.

Diaphanography (DPG): Use of light to visualize breast masses; useful in detecting fluid-filled cysts; considered experimental.

Differentiated: In describing cancer cells, the less normal the appearance of the cell, the more poorly it is *differentiated* and the more aggressively it behaves

Discharge: As pertains to the breast, any fluid coming from the nipple, regardless of color.

DNA flow cytometry: See *Flow cytometry.*

DPG: See *Diaphanography.*

Duct: Structure in the breast through which milk flows to the nipple.

Ductal carcinoma in situ: Cancer cells that have not spread beyond site of origin in ducts in the breast.

Dysgerminoma: Rare type of ovarian cancer that originates in germ cells. See *Germ cells.*

Edema: Swelling.

Embryonal carcinoma: Type of ovarian cancer.

Endodermal sinus tumor: Type of ovarian cancer.

Endometriod adenocarcinoma: Type of ovarian cancer.

Epidemiology: Study of the distribution and causes of diseases in human populations; can yield information on environmental influences.

Epithelial carcinoma: Cancer arising in the outer layer of the ovary.

Estrogen: A hormone, at higher levels in women, that has to do with sex differentiation.

Estrogen-dependent: A cancer that can grow only in the presence of the hormone estrogen.

Estrogen-independent: A cancer that does not require the presence of estrogen to grow.

Estrogen receptor (ER): Protein to which estrogen attaches; found on some cells.

Estrogen receptor assay: Test to determine if cancer is estrogen-dependent. See also *Estrogen-dependent*).

Excisional biopsy: Diagnostic procedure in which a lump

is removed from the breast to determine whether it is benign or malignant. See also *Incisional biopsy.*

External radiation: Radiation therapy delivered by a machine that aims high-energy rays at the area of the body where cancer was found.

Extraovarian papillary carcinoma of the peritoneum: See *Interabdominal carcinomatosis.*

False negative: Erroneous test result indicating that no disease is present when in fact it is.

False positive: Test result erroneously suggesting that disease is present.

Fat: A nutrient; high dietary intake is associated with increased risk of both breast and ovarian cancer. See also *Monounsaturate; Omega-3; Polyunsaturate; Saturated fat.*

Fibroadenoma: Benign breast tumor.

Fibrocystic disease: Benign breast condition unrelated to cancer risk.

Fibroid: Benign tumor of the uterus; also called myoma.

Fine-needle aspiration: Diagnostic procedure in which a fine needle is used to extract cells from a suspicious breast lump to determine whether it is malignant.

Flow cytometry: Technique used to measure amount and type of DNA in a tumor.

Free radicals: Unstable chemical substances capable of damaging normal cells and activating carcinogens.

Frozen section: Frozen slice of tissue that can be examined for cancer immediately after removal from body; results are not considered conclusive. See also *Permanent section.*

Genetic: Inherited or inborn.

Granulosa cell tumor: Type of ovarian cancer.

Grave signs: One or more symptoms indicating that breast cancer has advanced locally.

Grid: Device used on mammogram machines to intensify X-ray contrast.

Gynecologist: Physician who treats disorders of the female reproductive system.

Hereditary cancer: Pattern of cancer found in certain families; the risk for unaffected members can be as high as 50 percent.

Hormone receptor assays: Tests to see if breast cancer needs hormones to grow; determines direction of treatment (see *Estrogen receptor assay*).

Hormone therapy: A breast cancer treatment.

Hot flashes: Waves of body heat and flushing that occur with menopause.

Human chorionic gonadotropin (HCG): Hormone that, at elevated levels, may indicate presence of ovarian cancer.

Hyperplasia: Increased number of cells in a tissue or organ.

Hysterectomy: Removal of the uterus; sometimes the ovaries and fallopian tubes are removed at the same time.

Immune system: Network of organs, cells, and substances that defend the body against disease.

Immunotherapy: Experimental cancer treatment designed to stimulate the immune system to destroy cancer cells.

Implant radiation: Treatment in which radiation is delivered to site of cancer via thin plastic tubes temporarily implanted in the body.

Incision: Surgical cut.

Incisional biopsy: Diagnostic procedure during which a section of a suspicious lump is removed from the breast to determine whether or not it is malignant. See also *Excisional biopsy*.

Inflammatory breast cancer: Very aggressive type of breast cancer; breast becomes red and inflamed.

Informed consent: Process by which a patient is informed and educated about the benefits and risks of any medical procedure or study; physician may require patient to sign a document attesting to her understanding of those risks and benefits.

Initiator: Substance or stimulus that changes a cell to enable it to become malignant; further action by a cancer promoter is necessary to set cancer in motion.

In situ: In the site of; refers to cancer that has not spread.

Interferon: Protein produced in the body that in laboratory studies has shown some potential for treating cancer.

Interstitial implant: Container of radioactive material placed in body tissue for cancer treatment. See also *Intracavitary implant.*

Intra-abdominal carcinomatosis: Type of malignancy identical to ovarian cancer that can develop, for unknown reasons, among women whose ovaries have been surgically removed; also called extraovarian papillary carcinoma of the peritoneum.

Intracavitary implant: Container of radioactive material implanted in a body cavity, such as the chest or vagina, as part of cancer treatment.

Intraductal: Within the duct.

Intraperitoneal radiotherapy: A treatment for ovarian cancer in which a liquid containing radioactive phosphorus is placed in the pelvic and abdominal cavities to kill any cancer cells remaining after surgery.

Intravenous pylegram: An X-ray to evaluate the kidneys, ureters, and bladder; sometimes performed as a diagnostic procedure when ovarian cancer is suspected; requires injection of contrast medium to illuminate abnormalities on X-ray.

Invasive cancer: Cancer capable of spreading beyond the site of origin.

Invasive ductal carcinoma: Most common type of breast cancer; capable of spreading beyond the breast.

Laparoscopy: Surgical procedure in which a long, thin tube equipped with a tiny viewing device is inserted into the abdomen via a tiny incision; enables physicians to view internal structures and determine whether changes suggesting cancer are present.

Laparotomy: Abdominal surgery.

Lobes: Milk-producing glands in the breast.

Lobular carcinoma in situ: Abnormal cells within the parts of the breast capable of making milk (lobes).

Lumpectomy: Surgical removal of a lump and surrounding area of tissue.

Lymphedema: Swelling caused by excess fluid that collects when lymph nodes and vessels are removed by surgery or damaged by X-ray.

Lymph nodes: Glands that help defend the body against disease-causing organisms.

Magnetic resonance imaging (MRI): Imaging technique used to help diagnose disease by transmitting radio waves through the body. See also *Nuclear magnetic resonance* (NMR).

Malignant: Cancerous.

Mammogram: X-ray of the breast.

Margins: Tissue surrounding tumor. Must be examined for cancer cells.

Marker: Chemical changes, usually in the blood, that may indicate the presence of a particular type of cancer.

Mastalgia: Breast pain.

Mastectomy: Surgery to remove the breast. See also *Radical mastectomy; Modified radical mastectomy*.

Mastodynia: Breast pain.

Medullary carcinoma: Type of breast cancer tumor that appears encapsulated; prognosis is generally favorable.

Menarche: First menstrual period.

Menopause: Last menstrual period.

Metastasis: Spread of cancer.

Metastasize: To spread, as in cancer that has reached a site distant from its point of origin.

Microcalcifications: Tiny deposits of calcium in breast tissue; can be seen on mammograms; clusters may indicate ductal carcinoma in situ. Also called calcifications.

Modified radical mastectomy: Breast cancer surgery in

which the breast and axillary lymph nodes are removed; underlying chest muscles are left in place.

Monoclonal antibodies: Substances produced in the laboratory that can locate and attach to tumor cells in the body; can be used to deliver cancer-killing drugs directly to malignant cells.

Monounsaturate: Type of dietary fat; found in olive, canola, and peanut oil.

Mortality: Total number of deaths attributed to a specific disease.

MRI: See *Magnetic resonance imaging.*

Mucinous carcinoma: Type of breast cancer that contains mucus-producing cells; prognosis is generally favorable.

Mucinous cystadenonocarcinoma: Type of cancer arising in the outer layer of an ovary.

Mutagen: Chemical or physical agent capable of damaging a cell's genetic material; the genetic damage may be passed along during cell division and could lead to a malignant change.

Myoma: See *Fibroid.*

Myomectomy: Surgery to remove benign fibroid tumors of the uterus.

NMR: See *Nuclear magnetic resonance.*

Node-negative: No sign of cancer in lymph nodes removed from women with breast cancer.

Nuclear grade test: Assessment of how rapidly cancer cells are dividing.

Nuclear magnetic resonance (NMR): See *Magnetic resonance imaging.*

Nutrient: Food component that contributes to body growth and maintenance.

Obesity: Excess body fat; risk factor for breast and ovarian cancer.

Omega-3: Type of dietary fat derived from fish oils; may help lower the risk of breast cancer.

Omentum: Tissue connecting or supporting abdominal structures.

Oncogenes: Genes that when activated by carcinogens stimulate the proliferation of cancer cells.

Oncology: Study of cancer.

Oophorectomy: Surgical removal of the ovaries; also called ovariectomy.

Osteoporosis: Disorder in which bones become brittle, porous, and tend to break easily; occurs most frequently in postmenopausal women.

Ovariectomy: See *Oophorectomy*.

Ovary: Female reproductive organ in which eggs (ova) are formed.

Paget's disease: Form of breast cancer affecting the nipple; prognosis is generally favorable.

Palpation: Feeling the breast to detect abnormalities.

Papillary breast cancer: Type of breast cancer; prognosis is generally favorable.

Partial mastectomy: Removal of a portion of the breast surrounding and including the malignant lump; also known as segmental mastectomy.

Pathologist: Physician who diagnoses disease from studying tissue samples.

Peau d'orange: Skin puffiness over breast tumor; term is French for "orange peel," which is what the affected skin resembles.

Pectoral muscles: Muscles that overlay the chest and help support the breasts.

Pedigree: Family tree; genealogical information by which a family history of disease can be established.

Pelvic examination: Examination by a physician of female pelvic organs, including uterus, fallopian tubes, and ovaries; can help detect ovarian cancer.

Peritoneum: Membrane lining the abdominal cavity.

Permanent section: Slides made from samples of a tumor

removed for biopsy; provides definitive diagnosis of cancer. See also *Frozen section.*

Placebo: A harmless substance that may be substituted for a drug; when patients believe a harmless substance is a drug, they may derive physical benefit. In drug tests, some study volunteers are given the real drug, the others get a placebo.

Polyunsaturate: Type of dietary fat derived from vegetable oils.

Precancerous: An abnormality with the potential of becoming cancer.

Progesterone: The hormone produced after ovulation to prepare the uterus for possible pregnancy.

Promoter: Agent that acts on a cell previously exposed to a cancer initiator (see *Initiator*); both an initiator and a promoter are believed necessary for cancer development.

Prophylactic mastectomy: Removal of the entire breast to prevent cancer in high-risk women (see *Prophylactic subcutaneous mastectomy*).

Prophylactic oophorectomy: Removal of the ovaries to prevent ovarian cancer in high-risk women.

Prophylactic subcutaneous mastectomy: Removal of breast tissue under the skin and nipple to prevent breast cancer.

Prosthesis: An artificial body part; a breast form worn under clothing.

Psychoneuroimmunology (PNI): The study of the links between stress, emotions, personality, and physical disease.

Quadrantectomy: Removal of one-quarter of the breast.

Rad: Measurement of radiation dose; radiation-absorbed dose.

Radical mastectomy: Surgery to remove entire breast plus underlying chest muscles and axillary lymph nodes. Also called Halstead or standard mastectomy.

Radiologist: Medical specialist in performing and reading diagnostic X-rays.

RDA: See *Recommended dietary allowance.*

Recommended dietary allowance (RDA): Level of nutrient intake necessary to meet basic nutritional needs.

Reconstructive mammoplasty: Surgery to recreate breast after mastectomy. See also *Radical mastectomy, Modified radical mastectomy, Simple mastectomy.*

Regression: Shrinkage or disappearance of disease.

Relative risk: An estimate of risk calculated by dividing the incidence of a disease in a given population by the incidence among a matched group of people who do not develop the disease.

Remission: Disappearance of evidence of disease.

Sarcoma: Cancer arising in connective tissue.

Saturated fat: Type of dietary fat found in meats, dairy products, and other foods from animal sources.

Second look: Surgery to inspect the abdomen following treatment for ovarian cancer.

Segmental mastectomy: See *Partial mastectomy.*

Selenium: Mineral nutrient found in food.

Side effect: Symptom that develops as a result of taking a drug or having a medical procedure.

Simple mastectomy: Surgery to remove the breast but not the chest muscles or lymph nodes. Also called *Total mastectomy.*

Sonogram: See *Ultrasound.*

S phase fraction: Measurement of percentage of cancer cells dividing at any one time; determined by flow cytometry. See also *Flow cytometry.*

Staging: Determining the extent of disease in order to appropriately treat it.

Standard treatment: Medical treatment of proven effectiveness in current use.

Stromal tumors: Type of ovarian cancer arising in connective tissue.

Systemic therapy: Treatment that affects entire body.

Talc: A soft mineral, and the principal component of talcum powder; exposure may increase the risk of ovarian cancer.

Tamoxifen: Hormone drug used to treat breast cancer.

Taxol: Anti-cancer drug produced from bark of Pacific yew tree; shows promise as a treatment for advanced ovarian and breast cancer.

Therapeutic: Pertaining to treatment.

Total mastectomy: Also called *Simple mastectomy.*

Transvaginal ultrasound: A procedure in which a vaginal probe is used to conduct an ultrasound examination of the ovaries; further study is needed to confirm its usefulness in enabling physicians to detect early ovarian cancer.

Tubular carcinoma: Type of breast cancer tumor with microscopic tubular structures; prognosis is generally good.

Tumor: Abnormal mass of tissue; may be malignant or benign.

Ultrasound: A physical examination in which sound waves are beamed off internal structures to create a black-and-white television image; can distinguish solid tumors from fluid-filled cysts; used in diagnosing both breast and ovarian cancer.

Uterus: Womb; female organ in which fetus develops and is nourished until birth.

Xeroradiography: Type of mammogram.

X-ray: Radiation used in low doses to detect and diagnose diseases and in high doses to treat cancer.

Index

Adenocystic breast cancer, 53

Adjuvant systemic therapies, 143

Alcohol, and breast cancer, 16, 22

Alpha-fetoprotein, 99

American Board of Radiology, 93

American Cancer Society (ACS), 63–64, 74–75, 91–92, 183

American College of Radiology (ACR), 92, 184

American Medical Association, 91–92

American Osteopathy Board of Radiology, 93

American Registry of Radiological Technologists

American Society of Plastic and Reconstructive Surgeons, 184

Androgen, 109

Aneuploid cells, 132

Angell, Dr. Marcia, 127

Asbestos, and ovarian cancer, 21

Atypical hyperplasia, 30
link to breast cancer, 45
symptoms of, 44

Barium enema, 147

Benign mastopathy, 44

Bergvist, Lief A., M.D., 14

Beta carotene, 72–73

Bilateral salpingo oophorectomy, 149

Biopsy, 91, 95–97, 100–101, 129–132, 137

Bone scan, 134–135

Boston University School of Medicine, 13, 125

Breast
anatomy of, 41–43
development of, 42

Breast cancer
case histories, 111–121
gestation of 49–50, 102
stages of, 133–136
statistics, 5–6, 9–10, 18,

Breast cancer (*cont.*)
     24–25, 90, 91, 144–
     145
Breast cancer, diagnosing
  biopsy, 91, 95–97, 129–132
  cathepsin D test, 132
  DNA flow cytometry, 132
  estrogen receptor (ER)
     assay, 131–132
  mammography, 88–95
  nuclear grade test, 132
  physician's exam, 83, 88
  self-examination, 80–87
  ultrasound, 94, 95
Breast cancer, early detection
  mammography, 89–90
  statistics for survival, 133,
     136
Breast cancer, family history
     of, 23–24, 27–34. *See
     also* Breast cancer, risk
     of; High-risk groups
  and age, 30–31
  monitoring for, 33
  and prophylactic mastec-
     tomy, 106
  statistics, 29–30, 32
Breast cancer, onset of, *See*
     Carcinogenesis
Breast cancer, prevention of
  prophylactic mastectomy,
     106–107
  tamoxifen for, 146
Breast cancer, risk of. *See also*
     Breast cancer, family
     history of; High-risk
     groups
  and age, 9–10
  and alcohol, 16, 22
  and childbearing history, 7,
     8, 9, 22

  and diet, 11–12, 60–62, 65,
     66–67, 74
  and estrogen, 7, 8, 9, 11,
     12, 14–15
  and exposure to sunlight,
     17–18
  and menstrual history, 7, 8
  and obesity, 10–12
  and oophorectomy, 7, 8
  and oral contraceptives, 12–
     13
  and puberty, 8–9
  and radiation, 16–17
  and vitamin D, 18
Breast cancer, symptoms of
  breast lump, 103
  lymph node enlargement,
     50, 104–105
  skin changes, 103–104, 136
Breast cancer, treatment of.
     See also Cancer, treat-
     ment of
  adjuvant systemic therapies,
     143
  chemotherapy, 104–105,
     143–145
  hormone therapy, 143, 144,
     145–146
  lumpectomy, 104, 137–141
  mastectomy, 81, 91, 104,
     137–141
  radiation, 104, 140, 141–
     142
Breast cancer, types of
  adenocystic, 53
  carcinosarcoma, 53
  inflammatory carcinoma, 53
  invasive ductal carcinoma,
     52, 53, 130
  invasion lobular carcinoma,
     53

medullary carcinoma, 52
mucinous carcinoma, 52,
130
Paget's disease, 53
papillary breast cancer, 53,
130
tubular carcinoma, 52, 130
Breast lumps, benign
aspiration of, 46—47, 95—96
cysts, 46—47
fibroadenomas, 47
fibrocystic disease, 44—46
statistics, 78—79
Breast pain, 42, 44
treatment of, 45—46
Breast X-ray. *See* Mammography
phy
Breast, precancerous conditions
ductal carcinoma in situ,
51—52
lobular carcinoma in situ,
50—51
Breast-ovarian cancer syndrome, 35, 36
case histories, 111—115,
119—121
Brigham & Women's Hospital,
14—15

CA-125, 98—99
Caffeine, 45
California School of Medicine,
126
Calorie intake. *See also* Cancer: and diet, Fat intake;
Obesity
and breast cancer, 63—64
and cancer, 63—65
and onset of puberty, 64
Calorie tables, 157—176
Cancer

blaming the victim, 127, 128
metastatic tumors, 56—57,
133—135, 136, 148
precautions against, 74—75
primary tumors, 57
statistics, 26—27
Cancer centers, by state, 186—
194
Cancer, risk of
and diet, 26—27, 59—60, 62—
63. *See also* Calorie intake; Fat intake; Obesity
and emotional health, 122,
123—125
genetic predisposition, 7,
28, 30
and personality, 122, 126—
127
and smoking, 26
and stress, 122, 123—124
Cancer, treatment of. *See also*
Breast cancer, treatment
of; Ovarian cancer,
treatment of
laughter, 127
meditation and visualization, 127
Carcinoembryonic antigen, 99
Carcinogenesis, 73
and breast cancer, 49—50
mitosis, 49
Carcinosarcoma, 53
Cassileth, Barrie, 126—127
CAT scan, 135, 147
Cathepsin D test, 132
Chemotherapy, 104, 105, 143—
145, 150, 151
Childbearing history
and breast cancer, 7, 8, 9, 22
and ovarian cancer, 19
Chronic cystic mastitis, 44

Cisplatin, 151
Clinical trials, 152, 153
Colditz, Graham A., M.D., 14–15
Corpus luteum cysts, 56
Cyclic pronounced breast disease, 44
Cyclophosphamide, 151
Cysts. *See* Breast lumps, benign; Ovarian growths, benign
Cytotoxic, 143, 144, 145

Devitt, J.E., M.D., 78–79
Diet, and cancer, 11–12, 20–21, 26–27. *See also* Calorie intake; Fat intake
Diploid cells, 132
Directory of Medical Specialists, 78
DNA flow cytometry, 132
Doxorubicin, 151
Ductal carcinoma in situ, 51–52

Emotional health, and cancer, 122, 123–125
Endodermal sinus tumor, 99
Epithelial cancer, 57–58
Estrogen receptor (ER) assay, 131–132
Estrogen replacement therapy
  and breast cancer, 14–15
  to prevent heart disease, 8, 14, 15
  and lifespan, 14
  and oophorectomy, 8, 38
  to prevent osteoporosis, 8, 14, 15, 108–109
  for postmenopausal women, 13, 15
Estrogen, and breast cancer, 7, 8, 9, 11, 12

Experimental drugs. *See* Clinical trials

F. Lee Moffitt Cancer Center, 11, 12
Fat and calorie tables, 157–176
Fat intake. *See also* Calorie intake; Cancer: and diet; Obesity
  and breast cancer, 60–62, 65, 66–67, 74
  and cancer, 59–60, 62–63
  cutting down on, 70–71, 177–181
  fats in foods, 69–70
  and heart disease, 65–66
  and ovarian cancer, 19, 68–69, 74
Fibrocystic disease, 44–46
Fibroid tumors, 37
Follicle-stimulating hormone (FSH), 54
Follicular cysts, 55, 56
Fox, Bernard H., PhD., 125
Free radicals, 63
  and cancer, 63, 73
Friend, Stephen H., M.D., 28

Garcia, Celso-Ramon, M.D., 108–109
Geer, Steven, H., M.D., and Morris, Tina, 126
Germ cell cancer, 57, 58, 100
Gilda Radner Familial Ovarian Cancer Registry, 34, 36, 185

Harvard Medical School, 21, 65, 68, 71–72
Harvard School of Public Health, 16

Harvard University, 20–21, 124

Health University Plan (HIP) of Greater New York Screening Program, 89–90

Heart Disease
  and estrogen replacement therapy, 8, 14, 15
  and fat intake, 65–66
  and obesity, 11
  tamoxifen for, 145

Hereditary Cancer Institute, 32, 34, 113, 114, 119, 185

Hexamethylmelamine, 151

High-risk groups. *See also* Breast cancer, family history of; Ovarian cancer, family history of
  monitoring of, 76–77
  choosing a physician, 77–78

Hormone therapy, 143, 144, 145–146

Hospital of the University of Pennsylvania, 108, 109

Human chorionic gonadotropin, 99–100

Hysterectomy, 76, 149

Immunoglobin A, 124

Inflammatory breast cancer, 53

International Federation of Gynecology and Obstetrics, 147–148

Intra-abdominal carcinomatosis, 40, 115

Intraductal papillomas, 48

Intraperitoneal radiotherapy, 150

Intravenous pyleogram. *See* IVP

Invasive ductal carcinoma, 52, 130

Invasive lobular carcinoma, 53

Iridium, 141

IVP (intravenous pyleogram), 147

Johns Hopkins University, 124

Journal of Prospective Techniques [1957], 123

Journal of the American Medical Association [August 31, 1989], 125

King's College Hospital, 126

Klopfer, Bruno, M.D., 123

Klurfield, David M., M.D. 63, 64

Krebiozen, 123

Laparoscopy, 100–101

Laparotomy, 100–101

Li-Fraumeni syndrome, 28

Liver disease, 99

Liver scan, 135

Lobular carcinoma in situ, 50–51

Longnecker, Matthew P., M.D., 16

Low-fat diets, 177–181

Lumpectomy, 104, 137–141

Lung cancer, 6–7, 26

Luteinizing hormone (LH), 54

Lymph nodes, 50, 104–105, 138

Lynch, Henry T., M.D., 32, 114

Magnetic resonance imaging. *See* MRI

Malpractice suits, and breast
     cancer, 79–80
Mammary dysplasia, 44
Mammography, 88–95
  and age, 89
  and early detection of breast
     cancer, 89–90
  limitations of, 88–89
  recommendations for hav-
     ing, 45, 91–92
  risks of, 90–91
  standards for radiologists,
     92–93
Massachusetts General Hospi-
     tal, 28
Mastectomy, 76, 81, 91, 104,
     137–141
  prophylactic, 33–34, 106–
     107
Mastitis, 48
McClelland, David, Ph.D., 124
Medical research studies, 9–
     17, 20–22, 28, 30–32,
     34, 36, 39, 63–66, 68,
     71–72, 74–75, 78–82,
     89–92, 108–109, 113–
     114, 119, 123–127, 137,
     144–148
Meditation and visualization,
     127
Medullary carcinoma, 52
Metastasis, 133–135, 136
Metastatic tumors, 56–57,
     133–135, 136, 148
Metropolitan height and
     weight tables, 182
Microcalcifications, 138
Milan, Albert R., M.D., 82
Minerals and breast cancer
     selenium, 71–72
Monoclonal antibodies, 151

Mount Sinai School of Medi-
     cine, 124
MRI (magnetic resonance im-
     aging), 135
Mucinous carcinoma, 52, 130

National Cancer Institute
     (NCI), 13, 66, 91–92,
     146, 183–184
National Cancer Institute of
     Canada, 17
National Institutes of Health,
     137, 144–145
National Institute on Aging,
     125
New England Journal of Medi-
     cine [1985], 127
Nipple disorders
  intraductal papillomas, 48
  mastitis, 48
  subareolar abcess, 48
Nuclear grade test, 132

Obesity. See also Calorie in-
     take; Cancer: and diet;
     Fat intake
  and breast cancer, 10–12
  and gallbladder disease, 11
  and heart disease, 11
  and diabetes, 11
  and menstrual patterns, 12
Oophorectomy, 37–38, 39,
     108–110, 149
  estrogen replacement ther-
     apy for, 8, 38
  and intra-abdominal carci-
     nomatosis, 40
  prophylactic, 107–110
Oral contraceptives
  and breast cancer, 12–13
  and ovarian cancer, 19

Osteoporosis, 8, 14, 15, 108–109
Ovarian cancer
  case histories, 111–115, 119–121
  stages of, 147–148
  statistics, 5–6, 18, 24–25
Ovarian cancer, diagnosing, 97–101
  barium enema, 147
  biopsy, 100–101
  blood tests, 98–100
  CAT scan, 147
  IVP, 147
  pelvic exams, 98
  surgery, 146, 149–150
  ultrasound, 98, 100
  X-ray, 147
Ovarian cancer, family history of, 23–24, 27, 34–40.
  See also High-risk groups
  monitoring for, 38–39
  statistics, 34, 35, 36
Ovarian cancer, prevention of
  prophylactic oophorectomy, 107–110
Ovarian cancer, risk of
  and age, 18
  and asbestos, 21
  and childbearing history, 19
  and cultural factors, 18–19
  and diet, 19, 20–21, 68–69, 74
  and fat intake, 19
  and infertility, 20
  and menstrual history, 20
  and oral contraceptives, 19
  and radiation, 22
  and socioeconomic status, 19

  and talcum powder, 21
  and transferase, 20–21
Ovarian cancer, symptoms of
  abdominal changes, 105
  enlarged ovary, 105
  vaginal bleeding, 105
Ovarian cancer, treatment of.
  See also Cancer, treatment of
  chemotherapy, 150, 151
  oophorectomy, 149
  radiation, 150–151
Ovarian cancer, types of
  endodermal sinus tumor, 99
  epithelial, 57–58
  germ cell, 57, 58, 100
  stromal, 57, 58
Ovarian growths, benign
  corpus luteum cysts, 56
  follicular cysts, 55, 56
Ovary, removal of. *See* Oophorectomy
Ovulation, 54

P32, 150–151
Paget's disease of the breast, 53
Pap smear, 76–77
Papillary breast cancer, 53, 130
Personality, and cancer, 122, 126–127
Physicians Data Query, 153
Placebo, 46, 123
Primary tumors, 57
Prophylactic mastectomy, 33–34, 106, 107
Prophylactic oophorectomy, 107–110
Psychoneuroimmunology, 123

Queen Elizabeth II Medical
    Center, 10, 12

Radiation, 16–17, 22, 104,
    140, 141–142, 150–151
  intraperitoneal radiother-
    apy, 150
  P32, 150–151
Reagan, Nancy, 140
Resource organizations, 183–
    185
Roswell Park Memorial Insti-
    tute, 9
Rush-Presbyterian-St. Luke's
    Hospital, 30–31

S phase fraction, 132
Schleifer, Steven, M.D., 124
Selenium, 71–72
Self-examination, breast, 80–
    87
Shapiro, Samuel, 13
Skin changes, and breast can-
    cer, 103–104, 136
Smoking, and cancer, 26
Stress, and cancer, 122, 123–
    124
Stanford University, 20
Stromal cancer, 57, 58
Subareolar abcess, 48

Talcum powder, and ovarian
    cancer, 21
Tamoxifen

and breast cancer, 145–146
  and heart disease, 145
  side effects of, 145–146
Taxol, 151
Temoshok, Lydia, 126
Thomas, Caroline, 124
Transferase, and ovarian can-
    cer, 20–21
Transvaginal Doppler Color
    Flow Imaging test, 100
Tubular carcinoma, 52, 130

Ultrasound, 94, 95, 98, 100
  transvaginal, 39, 100
University Hospital, Uppsala,
    Sweden, 14
University of Massachusetts,
    80–81
University of Ottawa, 78–79
University of Pennsylvania,
    126–127

Vegetables, cruciferous
  and cancer, 74
Vitamins, and breast cancer
  beta carotene, 72–73
  vitamin A, 72–73
  vitamin C, 73
  vitamin D, 18
  vitamin E, 45, 73

Willett, Walter C., M.D., 22,
    65, 68
Wistar Institute, 63, 64